FRENCH COUNTRY LIVING

A YEAR IN

Gascony

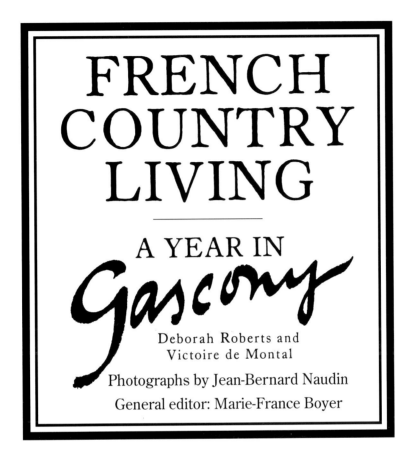

FRENCH COUNTRY LIVING

A YEAR IN
Gascony

Deborah Roberts and
Victoire de Montal

Photographs by Jean-Bernard Naudin

General editor: Marie-France Boyer

A BULFINCH PRESS BOOK

Little, Brown and Company

BOSTON TORONTO LONDON

For our children

First United States Edition

ISBN 0-8212-1826-3

Library of Congress Catalog Card Number 90-81596
Library of Congress Cataloging-in-Publication information is available.

Bulfinch Press is an imprint and trademark of Little, Brown and Company (Inc.)
Published simultaneously in Canada by Little, Brown & Company (Canada) Limited

PRINTED IN SPAIN

Important note: *All recipe measurements give the Imperial
amount first, followed by the metric and then the U.S. equivalent.
As these are not exact equivalents, please work from one set of
figures. U.S. teaspoons, tablespoons, pints, quarts and gallons
are all smaller than Imperial ones.*

    *Gardening instructions are all particular to Gascony. Plants
that can be grown and times for sowing and harvesting depend
upon local climates.*

CONTENTS

*'Men and women may sometimes, after great effort, achieve a
creditable lie; but the house, which is their temple, cannot
say anything save the truth of those who have lived in it.'*
RUDYARD KIPLING

Deborah Roberts

Victoire de Montal

This book is about two houses in Gascony, in south-west France, inhabited all the year round by two very different families.

Cosmignon, where Deborah Roberts lives with her husband and their two children, is in the south of the department of the Gers, overlooking the rolling clay farmland of Tenarèze. Deborah was born in Texas, and her husband, a writer, is English. She describes how they discovered the place: 'We had three days, a one-year-old son and another child about to be born. We bought this house; and though I wonder how we had the courage to do it when I look back at the old photographs, it was the happiest decision of our lives. A month later, a violent storm brought down part of the roof on the night of our daughter's birth; but we still had no second thoughts.'

Cosmignon is built of oak and cob, with a long roof of Roman tiles. It has the look of a mineral beast which long ago shouldered its way out of the ground, then, little by little, suffered its carcass to be dressed in the likeness of a human habitation. When Deborah first bumped down the hill to Cosmignon in 1977, the carcass had been uninhabited for a decade and was settling back into its mother clay, beneath a blanket of briars. Happily, the process was reversed by permanent occupation, and today this small farm is the sort of secret hideout many people dream about — ancient, utterly private, awkward to get to, and spectacularly ramshackle.

Arton, one hour away to the north, is something altogether different. Victoire de Montal and her husband Patrick are both Gascons born and bred. Victoire's brother is the present Duc de Montesquiou, and her family has played a leading part in local life and French national politics for nearly a thousand years.

Yet, like the Roberts family, the de Montals came to Gascony from Paris; they had dreamed of returning to live in the country of their childhood, and when they discovered Arton one day in August 1978, they seized the chance it offered.

Built in 1860, Arton is a graceful chartreuse, *or small country house, in pale limestone, surrounded by a huddle of outbuildings dating from the same period. The basic design – a common one in the area around the cathedral town of Lectoure – is that of the* plain-pied: *the high-windowed ground floor originally contained the entire living space, bedrooms included. The de Montals, who have two children of their own and four more from previous marriages, decided to convert the attic, part of the basement and some of the outbuildings. The conversion included a* chai, *or wine-making plant, for Fine Blanche, an unaged blend of Armagnac Patrick bottles and markets.*

'The house needed everything,' says Victoire. 'Bathrooms, electricity, heating and kitchen all had to be installed, before we could even begin to decorate. We quickly learned that restoring a house in the country is a very different proposition to fixing up a town residence.'

Like Cosmignon, Arton is married to the lie of the land. Lovely in colour and design, the house stands on the edge of a wooded hollow, protected to the north by a slight incline. Seen from the drawing room window, the field at the base of the hollow drops away to the bank of a pale green lake. Also like Cosmignon, the house is the centre of all, mothering the small farm and accepting the homage of the garden.

Many people in France, as elsewhere, have houses in the country where they spend the odd weekend or summer holiday. Many of these people dream one day of retiring to this second home when their working lives come to an end. But very few seriously contemplate forsaking urban life while they are still young, to exchange it for an apparently precarious and isolated existence in the countryside. Some do, and some succeed: hence the interest of this book, which is based on two families, one French, one Anglo-American, which are committed to life in Gascony from year's end to year's end.

Victoire de Montal and Deborah Roberts are sophisticated women who have travelled and lived all over the world, speak several languages and have a wide circle of friends. Yet for a decade past, their lives have centred on one of France's more remote provinces, where, had there been any truth to conventional wisdom, they should have been bored to death in a matter of months. As it is, after ten years, both feel that their existences have been enormously enriched. They have given their children a country upbringing; and they have learned much about a simpler and more innocent world. As Deborah and Victoire both say, the original decision was an obvious one; and it is that decision which was the origin of this book.

AUTUMN

SEPTEMBER

'A la Sainte Croix,   ON THE DAY OF THE HOLY CROSS
Cueille les pommes,   [SEPT. 14TH], PICK YOUR APPLES
Gaule les noix.'   AND BEAT YOUR WALNUT TREES.

I n Gascony one is torn all year round between the
mentalities of the ant and the grasshopper, but
never more so than during September. By mid-
month, all the children are back at school: Jack in
England, Savannah, Jean and Nine at Lectoure in
Gascony. Arton and Cosmignon are quiet again –
friends are gone and the nights are cool, the mornings
misty; but the midday heat can still be fierce. This is
the time when you can still bathe in the afternoon, yet
sit happily by a log fire after dinner.

In the early morning the meadows are covered
with dew-laden spiders' webs. Stubble fields, softened
by the first autumn rains, are transformed daily into
zen gardens of ochre ploughland. These days the
work is done by tractors, but Victoire can remember
when the ploughing was done by triple-harnessed
teams of oxen. September, with its opaline skies and
undercurrent of melancholy, can tempt one to lie
back, dream and do nothing while the last of the
summer ebbs away. The vegetable garden and the
hedgerows, however, are at their peak of abundance,
and harvesting that abundance cannot be postponed.

*(Left) Bringing in cabbages for
the* garbure *(vegetable soup).
(Right) The first mushrooms of
the season.*

'And as by some vast magic undivined the world was turning slowly into gold.'

EDWARD ARLINGTON ROBINSON

Both houses are busy with the various conserves which will later brighten meals, not only during the coming winter, but also during the really lean months of early spring. Much of the cooking of Gascony relies on ingredients harvested and preserved in September. Abundant beans (huge fat white Spanish and Tarbais, enormous speckled red and black ones, flagolets, limas, and cocos) and tomato coulis (recipe, page 92) will remain staple fare until the following June. Jams of blackberry and fig must be made before the ripe fruit is filched by birds and wasps. Courgettes (zucchini) and aubergines (eggplants) are put up or frozen in the form of gratins (with a crisp cheese or breadcrumb topping), ratatouille (page 92) and purées (page 93). Vinegars are flavoured with herbs such as tarragon, dill and rosemary; unaged Armagnac is scented with sloes and bottled. Apples and beetroot (beets) are also harvested and preserved for winter meals.

At Cosmignon, September is a time for culling the various animals of the farmyard – tender rabbits, chickens and pigeons which have grown fat on home-grown grain and hay during the summer months. Young female ducklings are smoked (page 92). The larger drakes are kept for the *gavage*, or force-feeding, which begins with the first cold weather in October, after the white maize used in the process has been harvested. The various farmyard animals, though time-consuming and uneconomical, supply eggs as well as delicious meat for roasts, stews and soups throughout the year – not to mention the pleasure of their company through the seasons.

With the cooler weather, heavy dews and first autumn rains, the grass and flowers begin to revive. Lemon-yellow crocuses appear overnight, and pale mauve cyclamen carpet the ground. The last roses of summer, giant ivory yucca flowers, asters, China

*(Left) Splitting ash logs: ash is one of the few woods which burn equally well green or dry.
(Right) Ingredients for a classic* garbure *(vegetable soup): green cabbage leaves, potted duck, white beans...*

14

asters, black-eyed Susans and graceful Japanese anemones provide ample raw material for flower arrangements. Victoire, whose birthday falls at this time, lays her table with fine white porcelain intertwined with the scarlet tendrils of Virginia creeper and celebrates with a *marquise au chocolat* (page 93), a rich chocolate dessert, the recipe for which came from the cook at Marsan, her father's château.

If the conditions are right (warm weather ten days after heavy rains) September is the month for mushrooming. Chanterelles or girolles (*Cantharellus cibarius*), trompettes de la mort (*Craterellus cibarius*), shaggy ink caps (*Coprinus comatus*) and parasol mushrooms (*Lepiota procera*) are just some of the wild mushrooms to be found, but the real prize is the cep or penny bun mushroom (*Boletus edulis*). An early start is essential to beat the neighbours and the slugs. During a good mushroom season the

(Preceding double page) Garbure, *or vegetable soup (recipe, page 97) as served at Cosmignon.*
(Left) Coffee stays hot on the Aga.
(Right) An armoire holds Victoire's compotes, jams, and other conserves.

woods of Gascony are almost as populated as the Bois de Boulogne on a Sunday, and the searchers come from nearly as far away.

A good harvest prompts all kinds of culinary activity – a favourite September lunch at Cosmignon is cold curried apple soup, chicken with cep mushrooms, and blackberry sorbet (page 94). Roast pigeon with *foie gras* and *mesclun* salad (page 93), followed by figs and cream, is another favourite.

In general, September is the most industrious month of the year, and everyone in the two households is busy getting ready for winter. All the same, one can have the best of both worlds by choosing a golden afternoon to shell beans outside, while the crows call and the conkers fall.

OCTOBER

'A la Saint-Crépin, la pie monte au pin
La mouche voit sa fin, le bois se rentre enfin.'

BY ST CRISPIN'S DAY [OCT. 25TH] THE MAGPIE'S IN THE PINE
THE FLIES ARE DONE WITH AND IT'S TIME TO LAY UP FIREWOOD.

O ut come the gumboots, old tweed jackets, beatup trousers and sweaters. October is the month when everyone is off in the fields, revelling in the sharp autumn sunshine, walking, riding, grapepicking – or shooting. If the grape-harvest and the arrival of the migratory *palombes*, or wood pigeons, coincide, it can be disastrous, for at the first distant sight of these great wheeling flocks of pigeons, any Gascon worth his salt will down tools and reach for his shotgun. The fever caused by the coming of the *palombes* is known in the region as *'Le Mal Bleu'*, after the colour of the pigeon's plumage. True

(Left) Force-fed ducks, with their livers still intact, as they are sold in all the local markets at this time of the year.
*(Right) The quarters of duck (*confit – recipe, page 94*) and livers (*foie gras – recipe, page 94*) are packed in jars and sterilized.*

fanatics will crouch in their specially constructed woodland hides for twelve hours at a stretch, surrounded by live decoys, trembling with excitement as the air around them fills with the sighing of wings.

The October grape-harvest is one of the last remaining occasions on which one can see large groups of people working together in the fields of the Gers. Grape-picking is sticky, back-breaking work, which continues for a full three weeks without respite. Around Cosmignon, the white grapes are mainly used for the production of Armagnac, though many growers keep part of the harvest to make a simple farmhouse wine for everyday drinking. The rest goes to the local distillers, where the wine is put through a sort of double-boiler, something halfway between a pot still and a continuous still. Armagnac differs from Cognac in that it is distilled only once, at a much lower strength: 53 per cent as opposed to

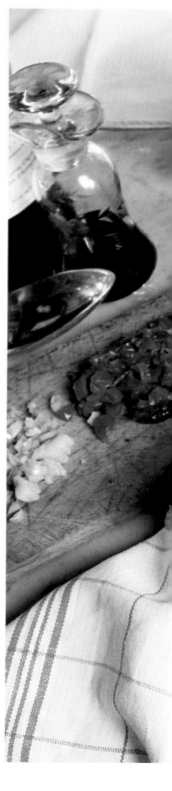

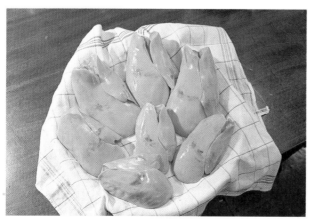

(Left above) Armagnac warms in a silver spoon before it is set alight and poured drop by drop over the pigeons (recipe, page 93).
(Left below) Duck livers, or foie gras, *freshly removed from the carcass, weigh around a pound (500 grams) each. For best results, they should be sterilized while still warm.*
(Right) All the ingredients necessary for roast pigeon with foie gras *and* mesclun *salad (recipe, page 93). A favourite at Cosmignon.*

Cognac's 70 per cent. This process leaves far more flavouring elements and scent than is the case with Cognac; to these is added the distinctive tang of the local black oak, used to make the barrels in which all Armagnac is aged. All year long the firm headed by Victoire's husband Patrick bottles and markets a special unaged blend of Armagnac, a delicious eau-de-vie known as Fine Blanche, which is drunk ice-cold like vodka.

At Cosmignon, the first spring hatches of ducklings are now ready for *gavage*, or force-feeding, and as soon as the weather is cool enough the process begins. The Muscovy drakes, after two weeks of force-feeding on cooked white maize, are turned into *confit* (potted duck, page 94), *magret* (breast of duck) and *foie gras* (duck liver, page 94). The skin and remaining morsels of meat are fried in duck fat for *fritons* and *demoiselles* (page 95) then eaten immediately and with relish. *Alicuit* (page 95), a rich stew made with the necks and wings of the stuffed duck, is frozen, to be eaten later with potatoes or polenta. The female ducks can be boned, stuffed with *foie gras* and sterilized in jars or used to make paté. With the prospect of all this rich food, now is the moment to try a *cure de raisins* (grape diet) for a few days, while the grapes are still plentiful.

Fragrant yellow quinces ripen in October and are made into quince jelly and quince cheese. At Cosmignon, Texan tradition requires that chopped jalapeño peppers be added to the jelly, to accompany roast lamb, while a wide variety of hot red chillies are harvested from the garden and strung up to dry. Jalapeños, which grow wonderfully in the Gers, must all be picked before the first frost and pickled or made into Mexican *salsa verde* or hot pickle (page 95).

Log fires are beginning to appear during the afternoons, and the rapidly shortening days invite gargantuan high teas of scrambled eggs, bacon, muffins (English muffins, page 95), scones (page 110), toast, butter and the freshly made jams of the season.

By now, provided the *palombes* have come in sufficient numbers (local lore has it that if they have not appeared by St. Luke's Day, October 18th, they never will) and provided the year has proved *cepeux*, or 'mushroomy', most locals are ready to face the winter without regrets. Once the grape-picking and winter sowing have been completed, there is little left to worry about but the maize harvest, which can be carried out little by little. Deborah concentrates on the garden, where she harvests pumpkins, decorative squash (coloquinthes) and chayote, and plants out spring bulbs. At Arton, the numerous walnut trees provide the raw material for Victoire's walnut bread (page 96) and sugared walnuts (page 96).

While most of Gascony feasts on *salmis* of pigeon (pigeon stew, page 96), Cosmignon celebrates Halloween, complete with grinning jack o'lantern and children in costumes. A favourite menu for this late October event is a mixed green salad with *fritons* of duck (fried pieces of duck, page 95) or fried cep mushroom stems, followed by tagine (Moroccan stew) of guinea fowl with quince (page 95) and a salad of oranges and pomegranate seeds (page 96).

The Gers is never more beautiful than in October. The pale autumn sun bathes the countryside in a golden haze; the distant landscape of rolling hills fades into deep blue, like the background of an Italian quattrocento painting. And then the wavering skeins of wild geese pass overhead: winter's on the way.

NOVEMBER

'A la Sainte-Catherine,   ON ST CATHERINE'S DAY [NOV. 25TH]
Tout bois prend racine.'   ANY TREE WILL TAKE ROOT.

T he Indian summer sometimes lingers well into November, with the occasional meal still taken al fresco; and then one morning one wakes to find the ground white with the first hoar frost. The air is crisp and clear and on the distant southern horizon, the snow-capped Pyrenees (invisible during the months of hazy heat) are etched against a brilliant blue sky. The first frost breaks up the heavy clay, which has not as yet become sodden with the winter rains.

For the farmer, November is the month for ploughing, harrowing, sowing, rolling and fertilizing. In the gardens of Cosmignon and Arton, the year's quota of new trees, shrubs, roses and perennials are planted out. Every year Deborah puts in a new Chinese tree peony, a species which does very well in the Gers – all the old farms have at least one. Another traditional Gascony farm tree is the shiny-leaved grenadine, or pomegranate, probably a vestige of the Moorish occupation during the Middle Ages. The bitter flesh of the local variety is sometimes used to flavour game.

With the first gust of wind after the frost, the trees are stripped and the ground becomes a patchwork of yellow, scarlet and copper leaves. The fireside is now irresistible. The chimney sweep has come by and permanent wood fires enliven the kitchens of both houses, which become the focus of all indoor activity with the arrival of chestnuts and *bourret*. The Gascon equivalent of vin nouveau, *bourret* is a milky grape juice drawn from the open fermenting vat. It is drunk for a period of about three weeks in November, while it changes from fizzy fruit juice to something approximating to wine. It makes a wonderful complement to chestnuts, roasted in a long-handled pan. In the old days *bourret* was the traditional drink used at Gascon *corvées* (heavy farm chores occurring seasonally) like the maize shucking, when the whole family would work around the fire together.

At Arton, Victoire begins making her own bread (page 99) around the beginning of November, a rite she will continue to perform until spring. Meanwhile, at Cosmignon, the earlier preparations for a Texas Christmas are in motion. The smoked ham has been ordered, the turkeys are nearing their prime, and the Christmas pudding (page 98) has been mixed. The flour tortillas, maple syrup, pecans and fresh gumbo filé (ground sassafras leaves, used in seafood gumbo) are on their way eastward across the Atlantic.

For the sombre feast of All Saints, which falls at the beginning of November, everyone in France who is able returns to his native village to visit family graves. The cemetery hedges are clipped, the grounds manicured and the graves covered with chrysanthemum blossoms a few days in advance. After the morning mass and the silent visit to the graveyard, a hearty, comforting lunch is much appreciated. *Gigot à la cuillère* (page 98) fits the bill – a leg of lamb simmered overnight with a pig's trotter (foot), then served with steamed mixed vegetables (potatoes, carrots, turnips, leeks) and stock reduced to thick gravy. This wonderful dish should emerge so tender that it can be eaten with a spoon, hence the name. Oysters baked in their shells (with a sauce of shallots, white wine and cream) make an excellent entrée, while a Camembert or Brie de Melun baked in a crust of croissant dough, followed by pears baked in red wine (page 98) served with crème fraîche should complete the warming of body – and soul.

Other essential November meals include *garbure* (page 97) – a local soup made with green cabbage leaves and *confit de canard* (potted duck) – and the classic Gascon *daube de boeuf* (braised beef stew, page 97), which is simmered in wood ashes to give a smoky taste. Traditionally, the top of the earthenware casserole used for the *daube* is sealed with a cabbage leaf. Up to 11 pounds (five kilograms) can be made at a time, and the longer the *daube* is cooked, the better it will be. In the old days, when all Gascon cooking was done on the open wood fire, housewives would keep their *daube* on the hob for days on end – as with *cassoulet* (Languedoc bean stew, page 106), another great regional dish.

Towards the end of the month, various practical precautions must be taken against the approaching bitter weather, since Cosmignon and Arton are both old houses and are vulnerable to sudden temperature plunges. As to the human inmates, a roaring blaze, a hot meal and a shot of old Armagnac are the best defences against the bite in the wind outside.

(Preceding double page) High tea by the library fire at Cosmignon: scrambled eggs, smoked cod's roe, toast, muffins (recipe, page 95) and homemade jams. (Above) Baked pears in red wine (recipe, page 98). (Below left) Muffins (recipe, page 95). (Below right) Ingredients for Christmas pudding (recipe, page 98).

WINTER

'Qui ne connaît pas la campagne l'hiver, ne connaît pas la campagne et ne connaît pas la vie.'

DRIEU LA ROCHELLE

A MAN WHO HAS NEVER KNOWN THE COUNTRY IN WINTER, IS A MAN WHO KNOWS NOTHING OF THE COUNTRY AND NOTHING OF LIFE.

DECEMBER

'A Sainte-Luce   AFTER ST LUCY'S DAY [DEC. 13TH]
Les jours avancent   THE DAYS LENGTHEN BY SLOW
du saut d'une puce.' DEGREES ('FLEA-HOPS').

Wherever the Christmas season is spent, it is the time of the year when everyone wishes they were a child again. At Arton and Cosmignon, children and adults alike are indulged to the hilt. Victoire and Patrick, who have six children between them, open their doors to their children's families and friends as well as their own close friends and often find themselves with as many as 18 at meals for weeks on end. When neighbours and their guests swell the ranks, delightful pandemonium prevails.

Feverish preparations fill the early weeks of December. Last minute presents must be found and wrapped. Boughs of pine, spruce, holly and juniper are cut in the nearby woods and placed on chimney pieces, on bookshelves and on the tops of cupboards to scent the house with Christmas. Branches of glossy magnolia leaves are arranged in large earthenware pots and placed here and there. Wreaths of bay leaves (page 102) are made for the door and also as gifts. Menus must be planned. Everyone pitches in to make goodies such as *truffes au chocolat* (chocolate truffles, page 101), mincemeat (page 102) for mince

(Left and right) The birds' Christmas tree (instructions, page 102) hung with suet balls and strings of wild berries and rose hips.

pies, fudge, divinity, caramels, gingerbread figures and lace cookies. At Cosmignon a turkey is home-smoked, and quantities of Creole sausage (page 101) are made and frozen for intermittent use during the holidays. This delicious spicy sausage is always eaten with oysters on New Year's Eve, and served as an hors d'oeuvre on other occasions, wrapped in croissant dough and baked.

It is only when The Tree is finally in place, however, that everyone heaves a sigh of relief and sits back to watch with pleasure Christmas's inexorable advance. At Arton the tree is a small live one that can be planted out in the scrub woodlands after the holidays. It is placed at the end of the central hallway on a round table covered with a beautiful old silk patchwork. It is watered regularly by Jean and Nine, who are in charge of its decoration as well as that of the crèche which surrounds it.

At Cosmignon a tree is chosen to reach the rafters of the upstairs drawing room, which is 14 feet (four metres) high. This is suspended from a cross beam with fencing wire, thus avoiding the prickly problem of stabilizing it at the base. A family expedition is mounted to find the *right* tree, overseen by the local forest warden. The tree selected must please everyone; at the same time it has to be taken from an area that is too thickly wooded, where other trees can grow the more vigorously for its absence. After much heated discussion, a candidate is chosen, felled and brought home with tractor and trailer. It is then laboriously manoeuvred into place, where, to the accompaniment of a roaring fire and frequent ladlings from the pitcher of hot spiced wine, everyone joins in with the decoration. Freshly made decorations such as silvered corn cobs and magnolia seed pods, popcorn garlands, gingerbread figures and candy canes are mixed with delicate old ornaments which are stored away carefully for use year after year. The tips of all the trees of former Christmases, labelled with their dates, are tied to the trunk of the new tree for good luck. Outside in the garden, Jack and Savannah always decorate a Christmas tree for the birds (page 102).

Each house has its special Christmas rites. For Christmas Eve, Victoire brings out her finest crystal and china and sets a sumptuous table, the decoration of which remains a secret until the doors of the dining room are thrown open. On the menu are a mixed salad of green beans, grapefruit, *foie gras*, lamb's lettuce and *mesclun*; stuffed turkey, purée of celery root and chestnuts; and plum pudding *flambé à l'Armagnac*. After Midnight Mass at the 16th century Lectoure Cathedral, champagne is served at home, with hot consommé (bouillon) and *feuilletés au fromage* (puff pastry canapés with cheese). Presents are placed behind the shoes around the tree, to be opened in the morning. On Christmas Day, after the presents have been distributed, a tremendous brunch is served. The table is loaded with brioches, tea, hot chocolate, cool white wine, home-made cherry and greengage-plum jams, toasted slices of country bread, patés, cheese and a delicious apple ice (page 102).

Christmas Eve at Cosmignon, by contrast, is taken up with frantic last-minute present wrapping (despite all attempts to be organized in advance) in every secret corner of the house. This is followed by a convivial dinner of Louisiana seafood gumbo (page 113) with steamed rice, corn bread (page 100) and a green salad. Finally, 'The Night Before Christmas' is read by the fire and candlelight, the stockings are hung, and the children are sent off to bed while their elders polish off the champagne and head for Midnight Mass at the village church.

The next morning a fire and candles are lit before the children are allowed upstairs to open their presents under the tree. Christmas lunch is Southern-style: home-grown turkey with cornbread stuffing (page 100), sweet potatoes mashed with orange juice, turnips puréed with their green tops, cranberry sauce, Stilton cheese, Christmas pudding with brandy butter (page 98) and Ambrosia (page 101. Ambrosia is an old Southern recipe for soothing the stomach after heavy eating and deep potation, such as always occur at Christmas.) The table is scattered with numerous small dishes containing an assortment of dried fruits and nuts, salted pecans, chocolate truffles, orangettes, fudge, Christmas

(Preceding double page) The Aga stove, heart of the house at Cosmignon.
(Right) Woodcock turning by the fire as their strings, or ficelles, *unwind (recipe, page 103). Below them, slices of toast spread with fresh* foie gras *catch the hot drippings.*

cookies, mincemeat pies and a centrepiece of Christmas roses in a silver jug.

New Year's Eve at Cosmignon is strictly intimate, for family and one or two house guests. Oysters and clams on the half shell are served with hot Creole sausages (page 101), followed by bouillon, *foie gras*, cheese, a *pastis gascon* (Gascony pastry, page 121), and – of course – plenty of champagne.

The *Réveillon* (Midnight Supper) of St. Sylvestre at Arton is sometimes a large party with orchestra and buffet and sometimes only family and a few friends. For a small gathering the menu consists of rabbit pâté, *oie de Guinée rôtie* (roast goose, page 100), *pommes dauphines* (dauphine potatoes, page 100), a salad of lamb's lettuce, Brie, and finally floating island (page 101).

Elsewhere in Gascony, the preferred New Year's Eve drink is the traditional local brew known as *brûlot* (page 102) – for initiates only.

JANUARY

'Janvier d'eau chiche   A DRY JANUARY
Fait le paysan riche.'   MAKES A RICH FARMER.

In the first month of the New Year, the Gascon weather oscillates wildly between downpour, hard freeze, impenetrable fog and clear, warm sunshine. Some days one is tempted to soak up the sun like a sleepy lizard, others to hibernate under feather eiderdowns with a good book. Nothing more can be done for the crops; these have now passed the ten-day danger stage of germination, when an entire seeding can be wiped out by a cold spell. By now, also, the ground is too wet for cultivation, so farmers turn to other tasks like wood-cutting, fencing, hedging and ditching. On Sundays, the local shooting associations organize noisy *battues*, or drives, around the woods and hills, until the strictly controlled annual quota of wild boar and roe deer has been filled. Following this a Breughelesque banquet of venison and wild boar is held in the village hall.

At Cosmignon, the Christmas festivities linger for a few days into January, with a lunch for departing houseguests and neighbours around the 2nd or 3rd of the month. The menu consists of cold smoked duck (page 92) and turkey with curried mayonnaise and champagne, a baked smoked ham (page 103), polenta soufflé (page 104) and ratatouille (page 92). This is the last major gastronomic event of the holidays; and even at Arton only the family is left by Epiphany (*la fête des rois*) to savour the traditional *tourteau*. The *tourteau*, or Twelfth Night cake, is a round brioche flavoured with orange blossom water and sprinkled with sugar; somewhere in it, a broad bean (fava bean) has been hidden. Whoever finds this bean in their slice of brioche is crowned king (or queen) with a gold paper diadem.

The Cosmignon Christmas tree is dismantled on Twelfth Night and makes a spectacular bonfire. The crêche and decorations are carefully packed away, and the children's minds are less on sugar plums than on the fast-approaching dates of their return to school. Jack, in particular, prays for snow like that of *annus mirabilis* 1987, when he was five days late getting back to England – much to the amusement of his schoolfellows, many of whom live in the frozen fastnesses of Scotland and Wales and consider the 'South of France' a tropical paradise.

No question but that this month of long nights is for living indoors. Communications by car are often seriously hampered by 'white-out', the sub-Pyrenean speciality of low, pea-soup fog made blinding by brilliant sunlight refracted from just above. In conditions like this, which can last for days on end, no Gascon in his right mind goes out in his car for any purpose other than essential shopping. Deborah, on her way to the village store in one of these terrifying fogs, once came suddenly on a giraffe and a camel, browsing by the cemetery hedge. A little further on a hippopotamus loomed from the swirling vapour. Seriously shaken, she was told by the boulangére that a tiny troupe of gypsy circus performers had chosen the village as wintering ground for themselves and their menagerie.

Reading, writing letters, needlepoint, mah-jong and cribbage by the fire are all pleasant ways to ride out January's storms. All sorts of household tasks that have been put off until a rainy day can be attacked now. Pure beeswax polish (page 105) and furniture reviver (page 105) can be made up and applied. Deborah transforms decrepit pieces of furniture by painting them with a mixture of natural pigment and rabbit-skin glue (page 104). Copper, pewter, and silver are all subjected to various special treatments at Arton under Victoire's watchful eye (page 108).

Meanwhile, the emphasis of the table has imperceptibly shifted to leaner, simple recipes: onions, potatoes and garlic come into their own. Onion soup, *tarte à l'oignon* (onion pie, page 102) and *confiture d'oignons* (sweet onion pickle, page 104) to accompany roast pork, appear. The onion skins are saved

(Left) The old kitchen at Arton, where lunch is served at pig killing time.

41

and boiled to make a rinse for blonde hair. This decoction was used by Venetian ladies of the 16th century, whose golden tresses were famed throughout Europe. Potato peelings can be soaked overnight and used as a rinse against hair loss. The potatoes themselves show up in any number of guises, such as leek with potato; spicy shepherd's pie (page 103); *galette de pommes de terre* (Gascon-style fried potato pancake, page 104); or a creamy gratin with its crisp golden crust. At Cosmignon, a standard January lunch is *tourin à l'ivrogne*, an ancient peasant dish of the region, in which an entire head of garlic, a little duck fat, seven cups of water, an egg, and a little salt and pepper are miraculously turned into a delicious, heart-warming soup. But best of all in January is the cooking of the open fire.

Before the days of electric stoves and gas ovens, all peasant cooking in Gascony was done directly at a wood fire – hence the huge grates and chimneys to be found all over the region, many of them tall enough for a man to walk into without bumping his head. The housewife's main cooking implements were her *crémaillère* (a hook and adjustable chain hanging from the back of the flue from which her cauldron could be suspended), her grill, her *landiers* (andirons) and her spitting irons, ladles and pokers. For this reason, one ingredient is common to all the great soups, *salmis* and *civets* (two types of game stew), *daubes* (braised meat dishes) and *grillades* (grilled food) of the region, and it is rarely, if ever, mentioned in recipes. This ingredient is woodsmoke, and in January it is available 24 hours a day, both at Cosmignon and at Arton. No wonder, then, that the majority of meat and fish consumed in both households during the month is grilled over the fire, or roasted beside it. Nothing compares with the flavour of a joint, basted and

turned before fresh coals raked forward every few minutes to keep the heat constant; or a *bécasse à la ficelle* (page 103) – a woodcock hung on a string from the chimneypiece – roasted and dripping over toast spread with fresh *foie gras*.

FEBRUARY

'A la Chandeleur   THE WINTER ENDS AT CANDLEMAS
L'hiver cesse ou prend vigeur [FEB. 2ND] OR ELSE BITES HARDER
Et la fleur de février   AND FEBRUARY BLOSSOMS
Ne vas pas au pommier.'   BODE ILL FOR THE APPLE CROP.

February in Gascony is a rainy month (*Pluviôse* in the French Revolutionary calendar), but already the days are perceptibly longer. On each successive clear evening the dusk holds off for slightly longer than one expects; and in the interval, for maybe three or four minutes, one senses the approach of spring. By the end of the month, the signs are clear; cones show in pine trees, dusty mustard-coloured catkins adorn the hazels, and yellow forsythias are in full flower around the farms. Crocuses and snowdrops begin to poke through in the garden, and in the woodlands dog's mercury, *bouton d'or* (lesser celandine) and wood spurge all make plain the fact that spring is on the way.

Meals in February continue to be simple and hearty. A particular favourite at Cosmignon is *poule au pot* (chicken in the pot, page 105) – the perfect way to dispose of an old hen who is no longer laying – served with small parcels of stuffed cabbage, Basmati rice baked in chicken stock, poached turnips, carrots, leeks and a sauce supreme. Winter salads made with red or white cabbage (page 108); lamb's lettuce and beetroot (beets); endive, walnuts and apples; or giant winter radishes and fresh anchovies (page 107) balance dishes such as *cassoulet* (Languedoc bean stew, page 106) or black bean soup (page 106). Dried pulses of all sorts (green, brown and orange lentils, chick peas, Tarbais, split peas, black beans and kidney beans) are especially appreciated at this time of the year. Seville or bitter oranges are in season, and Deborah begins to make her yearly quota of orange marmalade (page 107) while Victoire prepares tangerine jam (page 107).

The pig, whom the Irish call the 'gentleman that pays the rent', is normally killed in late January or February. For a year, he has been fattened on scraps from the kitchen, maize, barley and wheat from the land. Bought just after weaning at about 33 pounds (15 kilograms), he has by now attained the huge weight of about 400–450 pounds (180–200 kilograms), and the hour is nigh for him to 'lay down his life for France'. At both Arton and Cosmignon, the day of the pig killing is often set for early February, with the prospect of cool weather for at least six weeks longer. Cool air is essential for the process of curing sausages and hams, which might otherwise go off or fall victim to the flies of late spring.

(Left) The torteau, *or Twelfth Night cake, traditionally made for Epiphany.*
(Right) Roast goose (recipe, page 100) on the sideboard at Arton.

44

Ideally, the day of the pig-killing should be dry and cold. The *charcutier*, or pork butcher, who plies his trade around the farms of the district, is booked well in advance and paid a fee fixed by the préfecture. He is a man who has '*la main*' for the job, as the saying goes. And so he should, for to kill and butcher a pig efficiently in the traditional way involves considerable art, a sense of timing and above all economy of movement.

The ceremony of the pig killing lasts for two days, according to a pre-ordained schedule which never varies. On the first morning, after the pig is killed, bathed in scalding water, and scraped entirely free of bristles, the intestines are removed and cleaned with hot water; these will later be used for the sausage casings. The liver and kidneys are set aside to be eaten fresh or used in pâté, while some of the blood is cooked up like an omelette, with onions, bread-crumbs, garlic and parsley. This ancient Gascon dish, known as *sanguette*, is consumed by the company for lunch, along with a rich cut of meat from the neck, the *poux*, which is cut small and fried. By noon, the first stage is over; the pig has been split and is left to hang till the following morning.

The next day, the *charcutier* starts early and divides the pig into its various sections, each of which is destined for a different purpose. Mountains of meat rise on the tables; the bulk of it, which will be used for sausages (page 107) and pâté (page 107), is seasoned with pepper, salt, various spices and sometimes a dash of Armagnac or red wine. The pâté is sterilized in jars. The hams are set aside for salting; the fat is boiled off for storage in earthenware jars; and the chops, cutlets, roasts, ribs and feet are wrapped and frozen, or else salted down. Fresh sausages for drying in long loops; short sausages, peppered on the outside and tied at each end with white string; rolled belly meat; and the famous *coppa*, an intricately tied block of meat which will dry to a consistency not unlike beef jerky, are now all hanging neatly from rafters in a cool, dry place. Meanwhile the hams have been salted down with rough sea salt in a barrel. Here they will remain for thirty to forty days, being turned over from time to time, before being tied in white muslin bags and hung up to age.

Thus ends the pig-killing, an event of major importance, anxiously awaited and carefully planned. If all goes well, these two days of work will supply an abundance of meat in many delicious forms, for use throughout the coming year. For, as the Gascons say, the only parts of a pig you can't eat are the bristles and the teeth.

The religious festival of *Chandeleur* (Candlemas) occurs in early February, and may coincide happily with the sudden abundance bestowed by the pig – hence an excuse for a party. Formerly, the peasant custom in Gascony was to wrap a piece of gold in the traditional pancake, or '*crêpe de Chandeleur*', and toss it on top of the cupboard – where, if left for the whole year, it would confer prosperity on the household. But experience has shown that this method is not necessarily effective.

(Preceding double page) The Christmas table at Arton. (Left) Île flottante, *or floating island (recipe, page 101). (Right) Iced water and mint cordial: a charming detail in one of Victoire's guest bedrooms.*

SPRING

'Nothing is so beautiful as spring – When weeds, in wheels, shoot long and lovely and lush'

GERARD MANLEY HOPKINS

MARCH

'Mars pluvieux   A RAINY MARCH
An disetteux   A LEAN YEAR
Mars au soleil   A SUNNY MARCH
An plein de miel.'   A FAT YEAR.

March in Gascony, like October, is a month of intense effort. The farmers are once again racing against time and the fitful, sometimes stormy weather to finish the spring sowing. In the house the log fires are burning low, and soon the fireplaces will be swept clean and the last ashes spread in the flower

and vegetable gardens. From time to time, windows and doors are thrown open to let in the sunshine. By early April the carpets are out on the ground while the house undergoes the primitive ritual of spring-cleaning.

Outside, there is mounting excitement. The fields are greening over, the air on some days in early March carries a salt tang of the sea, and soon the swallows will be back in the great barn cut into the quarry face at Arton.

The first warm days are the time for long foraging walks with penknife and basket. Deborah comes home with dandelion and violet leaves for salads (page 109), dandelion buds for delicious omelettes (page 109) and fresh nettletops for soups (page 109).

(Left) Wild asparagus and leeks, oyster mushrooms, purple artichokes, peas, poppies and dandelion greens from the garden and fields around Cosmignon.
(Right) Savannah in the spring grass.
(Following double page) The pond at Arton in early spring.

These plants all have a high content of Vitamin C; they satisfy a craving for fresh green food as well as the springtime urge for physical purification.

Meanwhile, the steep sandy banks of a small stream running through the woods of Lupiac are the goal of an annual pilgrimage for the children; this is where the cowslips grow. More than at any other time of the year, wildflowers in March have the power to move us deeply. Snowdrops, violets and primroses are normally the first flowers whose names we learn in childhood. In the Gers, the Roberts children wait for violets to appear in the sunken lanes, along with the small roadside daffodil, the cuckoo-pint or '*pain de serpent*', and even the strange, medicinal lungwort with its pink and blue flowers. Soon the orchard at Arton will be in full bloom, the woods of Gascony rife with wild cherry blossom and the hedges tufted with the plum-scented blossoms of sloe (blackthorn).

March is the last month for pruning vines and many roses; the last month for buying and installing the year's pig; the last month for planting potatoes; the last month for purchasing young hens from outside, to bring new blood and supply eggs at the end of the summer when the old hens have completed their laying cycle.

With so many reasons to be out in the open, the kitchen tends to take second place in the scale of priorities, and consequently the dishes of the season do not, as a rule, demand long preparation. Such is

(Left) The peonies in the garden and (right) with lilacs in the salon at Arton.
(Page 59) A portrait of Victoire's mother, the Duchess of Montesquiou.

the case with the delicious *cassoulette de piballes* (page 109), with olive oil, garlic and hot chilli peppers – the *piballes*, or elvers (baby eels) from the Atlantic estuaries of Southern France are a wonderful local delicacy.

Another superb dish only available in March and early April is an omelette made with diced potatoes and tender young garlic shoots, or *ailettes*, from the garden: for some curious reason, the resulting omelette (page 110) has a taste and aroma comparable to that of cep mushrooms, which is probably why it is so prized in the mushroom-loving households of Cosmignon and Arton.

The last winter vegetables must be lifted from the garden at this time, to make room for the new seedings, so a regular feature of March menus is the all-encompassing *gratin de légumes* (vegetable gratin, page 109), in which carrots, fennel, Swiss chard, turnips, celery root, parsley, chervil and any other survivors are combined with stored potatoes and onions and a thick cheese sauce. This makes a tremendous accompaniment to a herb-scented *lapin en papillotes* (rabbit baked in parcels, page 110).

March is the time for spring tonics and all sorts of herbal preparations for health and beauty (page 111). It is also inexplicably the time of year when the children of both households yearn to cook. They are promptly set to work making pound cakes (page 111), scented with orange or lemon peel or with wild cherry flavoured Armagnac; those not eaten immediately can be frozen for summer teas. Other favourites include gingerbread (page 111), *merveilles de Marsan* (page 111) and scones (page 110).

La fête des Rameaux (Palm Sunday) often falls in March. At Arton, Victoire gathers branches of bay to be blessed during High Mass in the Lectoure Cathedral. Later they are brought home to replace those of the year before, in every room and outbuilding; this ancient custom is supposed to bring good luck and protect the house from harm until the following spring. Another Palm Sunday tradition acknowledged in the Gers and throughout rural France is the assumption that the wind which blows during the mass, or *messe des Rameaux*, will prevail throughout the year.

APRIL

'*Avril pluvieux*   RAINY APRIL/SUNNY MAY
Mai soleilleux   BRING HEART TO THE FARMER
Rendent le paysan orgueilleux   AND TROUBLE TO
Et l'usurier soucieux.'   THE MONEYLENDER.

In Mediaeval calendars, April was represented by a young man in green, with a garland of myrtle and hawthorn buds; in one hand primroses and violets, in the other the sign of Aries. There could hardly be a more apt image of Gascony at the beginning of this delicious month, which, though often cool and blustery, at last releases the blossoms and deep greens of spring. The old French maxim '*En Avril/ne te découvre pas d'un fil*' has its exact counterpart in the English 'Ne'er cast a clout/till April's out', and even this far south the advice is sound. For April is a month to be out in the open all day, preparing and sowing the vegetable garden, or exploring, by car or bicycle, the remoter corners of the Gers. April is also the time of year to hunt for *roumillous* (wild asparagus, page 112), *poireaux des vignes* (wild leeks, page 112), and *mousserons* (St George's mushrooms, page 112).

Mousserons are the most delicate and delicious mushrooms imaginable. Their odour is unmistakable yet indescribable; the scents of jasmine, cucumber, freshly ground flour and wet leaves have something to do with it. 'Fresh' is the adjective that most readily springs to mind. *Mousserons* are to be found year after year in roughly the same spot, though they are known to 'walk' a short way occasionally, and will disappear for ever if any chemical fertilizer reaches their habitat. They grow in the most inaccessible thickets where no one would ever attempt to penetrate were it not for the hope of discovering an unplundered *mousseronière*. Every farm has one or two of these secret woodland places where the *mousserons* come back year after year. As for their preparation, the simplest method is the best. Sometimes they do not even reach the table, as they are delicious raw, eaten on the spot as soon as they are

picked. They are particularly good in omelettes as they have the same ability as truffles to pervade eggs with their aroma.

The first bluebells, lilacs, irises, hawthorn blossoms and sometimes even a few peonies appear around Deborah's birthday, on the 7th of the month. This is a major family occasion at Cosmignon, when a Louisiana seafood gumbo (page 113) is ritually devoured. Seafood gumbo requires long and careful preparation and special ingredients such as filé powder (ground sassafras leaves), okra, Creole sausage (page 101), shrimp, crab and oysters. April being the last month with an 'R' in it, the local Arcachon oysters are already creamy and best eaten hot in this way. A frozen chocolate mocha mousse (page 114) completes the meal.

Easter, the date of which varies from the end of March to mid-April, is also a time of festivity, particularly at Arton, where Victoire welcomes the year's first major crop of guests. The children in both households go to infinite pains to decorate hens' eggs for the traditional Easter egg hunt in the garden. Some of their creations are so carefully wrought that calamity results if they are hidden and then not found. Savannah has perfected a process in which eggs are boiled in spinach, beetroot (beet) or onion water, with leaves pressed against them by a muslin (cheesecloth) wrapper, thus printing the silhouette of the leaf on the surface of the eggshell.

Good Friday is observed in both households with a traditional *brandade de morue* (cream of salt cod, page 114). A typical Easter menu at Arton begins with salmon or sea trout marinated in Fine Blanche and dill, followed by roast sucking lamb, *pommes*

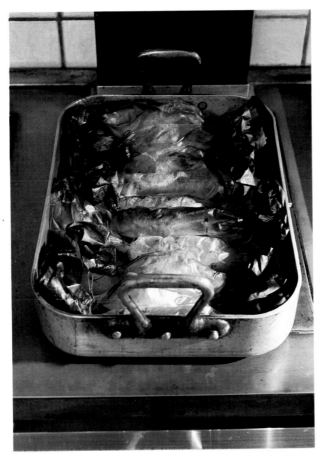

(Left) Deborah's seafood gumbo (recipe, page 113).
(Right) Lapin en papillotes, *or rabbit baked in parcels (recipe, page 110).*
(Following double page)
The celebrated pastis gascon, *or Gascony pastry, ready for the oven.*

(Left) Pastis gascon, *or Gascony pastry.*
(Right) Sorbet au chocolat, *or chocolate sorbet (recipe, page 116).*
(Page 69) Cocktails for a May evening (recipes, pages 117–118).

dauphines (dauphine potatoes, page 100) and a *pastis gascon* (Gascony pastry, page 121). Culinary wanderlust, a malady which often afflicts Cosmignon during the month of April, results in dishes such as Mexican tortilla soup (page 114) or stir-fried turkey breasts with pine nuts and chilli (page 113).

By mid-month, spring-cleaning is over and the house should now be spick-and-span. The final load of manure has been carted from the stable to the garden, and (weather permitting) the animals are permanently out at pasture. Once the farm has been inspected and the *mousseronières* scrutinized, one feels an urge to go further afield and see how the rest of the district is doing.

The Gers is full of ancient fortified villages, most of them unknown to any but the most enterprising tourists. As for châteaux, the department contains over two hundred, dating from widely different epochs. Thus the supply of fascinating places to visit is well-nigh inexhaustible, and April is the perfect time – before the heat is too great, before the nettles and briars have grown too high, and before the burgeoning trees obscure the towers in their midst.

Especially interesting are the rough lines of 12th and 13th century walled villages and castles that stretch along the rivers Baise and Gers. Some historians have attempted to see in these a deliberate defensive strategy on the part of the kings of England, who occupied the region for over two centuries; but the truth is that they reflect little more than the state of feudal anarchy which prevailed here.

At all events, few people, even locals, know the half of the extraordinary vestiges which may be found all over the countryside of the Tenarèze and Haut Armagnac. And when one tires of looking at old buildings, one can always drop into the nearest village restaurant, for a delicious lunch.

Finally, April is the month for the birds. Hardly a day goes by without a new hatch of ducklings appearing single-file from some hollow tree trunk, or a clutch of baby chicks tumbling from their nest in the straw. The hedgerows are aflutter with frenetic nesting birds. Along with the swallows, there are the nightingales, nightjars and cuckoos, which have returned from their African wintering grounds. If you have money in your pocket when you hear the cuckoo's plaintive chant, you'll be rich for the whole year – or so the saying goes.

MAY

'Mai frileux, an langoureux,   A COOL MAY, A SLUGGISH YEAR,
Mai fleuri, an réjoui,   MAY FULL OF BLOSSOMS, A BUMPER YEAR,
Mai venteux, an douteux.'   A WINDY MAY, A BAD YEAR.

Napoleon Bonaparte, on the subject of bullfighting in the Southwest of France: 'I don't give a damn if the Gascons get themselves killed, as long as they're having a good time.'

In May the Gascons do have a good time, but happily without loss of life ... though bullfighting is still very much a part of local tradition. Over the long holiday weekend of Pentecoste the local market town of Vic Fezensac hosts three days of bullfights which always attract top-flight matadors and informed afficionados. A short distance away, at Roquebrune, the ruins of a third century Roman temple, said to have been dedicated to the cult of Mithras, indicate that this ritual sacrifice of the bull has deep roots in the region.

With the long holiday weekends of May Day and Ascension also falling in this month, May at times seems like one continuous fête. Friends and relatives arrive to swell the ranks at Arton and Cosmignon. At last, *la belle saison* begins. The first tender young asparagus shoots are poking through in the vegetable garden, and broad beans, petit pois and tiny purple artichokes are ripe for the picking.

But it is the flowers that are the most enchanting aspect of the month of May. Vases, overflowing with bouquets of peonies, lilacs, irises, gypsophila and poppies, crowd every corner of the house. Horse chestnuts unfurl their sticky leaves and form canopies of white or salmon-pink. New roses bud and blossom by the hour in the first really hot weather. The south wall of Cosmignon foams with heavy-scented Albertine; Gloire de Dijon roses, the same dusky yellow as the cob walls, cover the front of the house. Among her many old-fashioned varieties, Victoire's favourite is a fragrant purple-red rose with a green button center. Like Albertine, many of these flowers only bloom in early summer and must be enjoyed while they last; and every May one gives thanks that the rose family grows so wonderfully in the otherwise difficult gardening soil of the Gers.

The wild ground orchid family also thrives in Gascony's heavy clay. The intricacy and variety of this threatened species are dazzling. One finds the fat-bellied early spider orchid, the pink-sepalled bee orchid, the white-scented butterfly orchid, the lizard orchid dangling its corkscrew streamers and stinking of goats, as well as the more common pyramid and soldier orchids. Sometimes one comes upon an abandoned water-meadow where as many as 15 different types are to be found, and in profusion. Unfortunately every year several of these magical spots fall victim to the plough. The guelder and dog rose that garland every country lane, however, seem in little danger of extinction.

Griottes, Guignes, Coeurs de Pigeon, Bigarreaux, Burlat, Montmorency, and plump Napoleons: May is cherry-picking time. Picking cherries is not without its hazards: climb too far out on a brittle cherry branch and you may find yourself in plaster for the rest of the summer. Birds, which can strip a tree in the blink of an eye, must also be outwitted. Once these obstacles have been vanquished, Victoire makes cherry jam (page 117), compote (page 116), cherries in syrup (page 117) and *clafoutis de cerises* (cherries baked in batter, page 117) with the spoils of her orchard. At Cosmignon, the wild cherries are preserved in Armagnac (page 116). Broad beans are picked and prepared for the freezer at this time. Asparagus are peeled and bottled, tips up, in salted water.

Meals taken inside the house are now the exception rather than the rule. Hammocks are hung for afternoon naps. With the lengthening twilight hours one's thoughts turn readily to cool and soothing summer drinks such as a mint julep (page 117), Pimm's (page 118) or white Emmanuelle (page 118). Menus are planned around the delicious spring vegetables at hand. Poached lambs' brains (page 115), served with steamed baby turnips, carrots, peas, spring onions and new potatoes and topped with a sauce of cream, fresh herbs and orange juice, embodies the delicacy of May. Soup with ham-filled omelette (page 115), which is made with tender broad beans (fava beans) from the garden and an omelette-like pancake of eggs, ham and garlic, is a hearty local speciality. A typical meal for Ascension Day or Pentecoste begins with a salad of cockles and broad beans (page 116) followed by rabbit with artichoke hearts (page 116) and a chocolate sorbet with Fine Blanche (page 116) for dessert. On days when nobody feels like cooking, the children are quite content to disappear till nightfall with a fishing rod and a *baguette* full of ham and cheese.

SUMMER

'Two hundred loaves of bread, and an hundred bunches of raisins, and an hundred of summer fruits, and a bottle of wine....'

BOOK OF SAMUEL II: xvi;i

JUNE

'Un pré est bien vaurien   A FIELD IS WORTHLESS
Quand en juin, il ne donne rien.'   THAT YIELDS NOTHING IN JUNE.

The colour of June is dark green, the smell of it is new-mown grass, and the dominant sound is the stridulation of crickets. This is the month for swimming, picnics and long dinners out-of-doors under the lime (linden) trees; the month for bullfrogs, bats, glow-worms, moths, lizards and snakes; the month for short starry nights and sudden violent thunderstorms. The farmers, anxious to complete their first cut of hay as early as possible (the earlier the hay, the better its quality and nutritive value), agonize about the uncertain weather. The children, oppressed by exams, pine for the holidays which begin at the end of the month. In the Southwest of France, summer starts more or less punctually at the beginning of July, the temperature climbs steeply, the capricious rains cease, and drought sets in till at least the end of August. Knowing this, anyone who has flowers, fruit trees or a vegetable garden will be busy with many tasks in June.

By coincidence, the outside tables of Cosmignon and Arton are both set under spreading lime (linden) trees, with the result that both families take most of

(Right) The porch at Cosmignon.

72

their June meals beneath a yellow, bee-filled canopy of blossom. At the moment of flowering, the blossoms are carefully picked (with their helicopter-like under-leaves) and dried to use for infusions (page 122). Sage, thyme, mint, and lemon verbena are also gathered and stored. Rose petals are picked and dried for pot-pourri and rosewater and lavender flowers for scented posies (all on pages 122–123).

In the garden, the work is half sowing, half harvesting and all weeding. Sweet corn and the entire bean family should be in the ground by mid-June. By way of reward, a few precious new potatoes can be lifted, and the first soft fruits – apricots, strawberries and raspberries – should be ready for picking. When one gets over the novelty of all this delicious fresh fruit, the excess goes for jams, pies and puddings. Pea soup with mint (page 120), roast duckling (page 120) with new potatoes, followed by summer pudding (page 121), constitute a standard meal for the season.

June is an excellent month for snail hunting. 'Follow, for he is easy-paced, this snail,' says John Donne, 'Be thine own palace, or the world's thy gaol.' The *escargot de vigne* (vineyard snail) or *petit gris* (grey snail) is pursued at night, immediately after a

(Preceding double page) Breakfast on the porch at Cosmignon.
(Left) A favourite summer snack: croûtons grillés à la tomate, *or toasted country bread with chopped tomatoes, garlic, basil and olive oil (recipe, page 127).*
(Right) Summer meals are eaten under the lime (linden) tree.

heavy rainstorm, and on a suitable evening a child with a torch (flashlight), a raincoat and a pail can gather hundreds at a time along the hedges and roadsides. Nobody who has not done this can imagine how exciting it can be. While the weather is dry, snails hide in secret places under logs, behind stones and in piles of vegetation. They are seen so rarely under ordinary circumstances that one is unprepared for the armies of glistening creatures that show up in the torchlight, simultaneously wakened by the wet.

Once gathered, the snails must be caged and carefully fed before they can be cooked. An *escargolade*, or snail feast, is the focal point of the fête at a village near Cosmignon. A thousand or so snails are cleaned and poached in a herb-filled consommé (bouillon), then tossed and sautéed with basinfuls of chopped parsley, garlic and breadcrumbs. Snails cooked with a delicate whisky-flavoured stuffing (page 119) make a dish of extraordinary refinement; at the other end of the spectrum, believe it or not, they can be roughly grilled and then eaten cold with raw garlic, salt and fresh bread. A much-revered neighbour of the Roberts used to relish this fare for breakfast, washing it down with black coffee and Armagnac.

Any excuse is good for a picnic in June. Southern fried chicken (page 120), potato salad (page 119) and devilled eggs (page 119) are old favourites at Cosmignon. Cold chicken, home-made potato chips and *tarte aux fraises* (strawberry tart, page 120) are the fare at Arton, where Nine and Jean host a yearly picnic beside the lake to celebrate the end of school.

On June 24th, St. John's Day, garlic is traditionally harvested. It is left to dry in the sun and later braided into the thick ropes which hang in every Gascon kitchen throughout the year. A fitting main course for this day is the classic chicken with forty cloves of garlic (page 120). A delicate *pastis gascon*, the region's most celebrated pastry, makes a perfect complement to this formidable dish. At nightfall, bonfires (*'les feux de Saint Jean'*) are lit all over the countryside, each farm vying with the next to produce the most impressive blaze. Dances are held in the light of the flames, and the children count how many fires they can see glimmering across the valleys.

JULY

'*Si juillet est beau*   IF JULY IS FINE
Prépare les tonneaux.'   MAKE READY THE WINE-BUTTS.

July is the laziest month of the year. It is also, alas, haymaking and harvest time. The sun beats mercilessly down, the ground hardens and cracks, and cattle huddle in the shade. Bringing in the bales of straw and hay in such heat is a job nobody relishes – one would far rather doze by the pool, or read a book in the darkened library. Yet it has to be done.

At Cosmignon, huge pitchers and thermos flasks of old-fashioned lemonade (page 125), cold spiced tea (page 125) and icy beer are stored by the hedge and freely imbibed. Lunch, which is set in the cool, shuttered house, consists of pâtés and conserves from the previous winter: country-cured ham, pork and duck pâtés, stuffed ham hock and cold *confit* of duck, goose or pork, with home-pickled gherkins, red wine and the glorious *miche de pain*, a country loaf as big as a badger. Dinner, taken outside in the cool of the evening, might include a Spanish tortilla (page 124) filled with onions, peppers, potatoes, tomatoes (the first from the garden) and herbs, followed by fresh peaches in wine.

Work in the garden, like everything else, has slowed perceptibly because of the heat and is mostly confined to the early morning and late afternoon. The blackcurrants are harvested and made into jams (page 126), syrups (page 126) and liqueurs (page 125); their tender leaves are used for infusions, or to scent delicate *sorbets* (sherbets, page 126). Likewise, the earlier plums and the greengages plums are fully ripened, ready for conversion into *confiture de menage* (mixed fruit jam, page 126) – a blend of greengage plums, mirabelles (cherry plums), peaches and apricots – and hot plum sauce (page 124), which is delicious for marinating barbecued spareribs. Just before the greengage plums ripen, they are preserved in Armagnac (page 125), a practice that is followed in virtually every Gascon farmhouse at this time of year.

Meanwhile, vegetables and herbs are growing apace, and sometime around the middle of the month the consumption of tomatoes, sweet peppers, melons, courgettes (zucchini) and aubergines (eggplants) begins in earnest. Basil, hot peppers and tarragon are put up in oil (page 123), and light wine is bought in bulk for bottling, in anticipation of guests who will arrive in August. An icy gazpacho (page 124) tastes marvellous about now. Seviche of tuna (page 123) and prawn (shrimp), cherry tomato and goat cheese salad (page 123) are other refreshing dishes which go well with the July heat. Creamed courgettes (zucchini, page 123) is a simple and delicious accompaniment to grilled or roast chicken, and peach cobbler (page 124) an irresistible ending to any July feast.

The entire atmosphere of the month is ruled by the harvest and the heat. Wheat, oats and barley ripen quickly in the blazing sunlight, and the huge combine harvesters go panting up and down the hills well into the night. At Cosmignon a ton or so of grain is kept back for the ducks, chickens and rabbits. Around Arton the melon harvest is in full swing. Lectoure is famous for its melons which are carefully selected for ripeness and hand-picked each day throughout the season.

Finally, July is the month of shooting stars and magnolia-scented nights, swimming and sleeping in the sun. The house is readied for August guests, but, in general, everyone does as little as possible. Even the *14 Juillet* (Bastille Day) passes quietly at Arton and Cosmignon, with only the occasional echo of distant fireworks to disturb the still night air.

AUGUST

'Août mûrit, septembre vendange,
En ce deux mois tout s'arrange.'

AUGUST IS FOR RIPENING, SEPTEMBER FOR PICKING,
IN THESE TWO MONTHS EVERYTHING FALLS INTO PLACE.

Holidays and August go together nearly everywhere, but in France they are indissoluble; from the first day of the month, the cities empty as if by magic and the countryside fills with visiting friends and relatives. Every village in the nation has its *kermesse*, or village fête, of a few days, but at Cosmignon and Arton the fêtes seem to last all month long. Luckily, August is not a busy time on the land, the hay and the winter crops having been harvested earlier. The vegetable garden should be more or less under control, and there is plenty of leisure to entertain visitors. By tacit agreement, the pace of existence is slowed for a while. Troubles and worries are pushed into the background, and the focus of things reverts to friendship and pleasure.

Breakfast is an informal affair, with everyone rising as early or late as they please, and making their own way through coffee, tea, jam and toast. After the pursuits of the morning comes a lazy midday meal under the lime (linden) tree, which will probably last well into the afternoon. Dinner comes late, Spanish-style, as the heat begins to wane – and is usually

(Left) Gazpacho (recipe, page 124).
(Right) A glimpse of roses – one of the guest bedrooms at Arton.

accompanied by a rising moon, flickering candlelight and a distant chorus of bullfrogs, toads and cicadas.

With so many mouths to feed, meals are kept simple and easy to prepare, always affording plenty of scope to accommodate unexpected arrivals. Everyone helps in the kitchen and with the chores. Recipes are gleaned from visiting cooks. The bounty of the vegetable garden – tomatoes, French beans (green beans), runner beans, white beans, salads, aubergines (eggplants), courgettes (zucchini), peppers, sweet corn and plentiful fresh herbs of every variety – and the abundance of fresh fruit like melons, peaches, nectarines and plums suggest the menus. If you are not content to exist on '*amour et eau fraîche*' (love and cold water) during the dog days of August, here are a few suggestions.

Pasta dishes are always popular. Pasta salad with tomatoes, basil and garlic (page 127) and aubergine (eggplant) pasta (page 127) are two particular favourites at Arton and Cosmignon. Cold soups such as Okrochka (chilled cucumber and yogurt, page 128), vichyssoise (page 128) and *soupe du mois d'août* (August soup, page 128) refresh and please the parched palate. Salads are an obvious and irresistible solution for August lunches. A mixture of squid, sliced onions and potatoes with an *aïoli* dressing (page 127), served when still warm, is delicious. Purslane and cod (page 129) are an unusual and pleasing combination. An enormous bagna cauda (page 128) with platters of raw vegetables or a gigantic *aïoli* (page 128) make messy but marvellous outdoor feasts.

When the weather is very hot, vegetables are much more appealing than meat dishes. A cold compote of courgettes (zucchini, page 129) or aubergine (eggplant) gratin (page 129) followed by

(Preceding double page) A breakfast tray at Arton.
(Left) Aïoli, or garlic mayonnaise, is served with sea-snails, vegetables, poached cod, squid, winkles and hardboiled eggs (recipe, page 127).
(Right above) Sébastien's aubergine (eggplant) pasta (recipe, page 127).
(Right below) The dining room window at Cosmignon.

cheese and fresh fruit is often all that is called for. Tandoori chicken served with corn on the cob and baked baby aubergines (eggplants), eaten with a dribble of olive oil, chopped garlic and parsley or an aubergine and yogurt purée (page 127), followed by watermelon ice (page 129) or chilled peaches in raspberry sauce (page 129) will delight even the most demanding gourmet. Sometimes simplest is best. For a light supper, midnight snack or August high tea, nothing is better than grilled (broiled) tomato croûtons (page 127), which is always in demand at Cosmignon and Arton and is often served with scrambled eggs.

French beans (green beans) are a blessing in the long term and a nuisance during the month of August. One never tires of eating them, especially in salads, but one quickly tires of picking them, which should be done at least every two to three days in the cool of the morning to ensure a constant and tender supply. The effort involved is well worth the treat of crisp tender beans in mid-winter. (As well as being blanched and frozen, French beans can be blanched in salted water then packed in jars in salt water. They are also delicious puréed with cream or butter.)

Every type of plum abounds in orchards, hedges and markets at this time as well. Guests are ruthlessly press-ganged to join in the picking for plum jam (page 129). *Vin de pêche* (peach leaf cordial, page 129), made with the tenderest peach leaves – which are traditionally picked on the 15th of August – is another conserve not to be forgotten. The 15th of August is the fête of the Assumption of the Virgin Mary, who is credited with the power on this day of making or breaking everything (*'La Vierge du 15 août, arrange ou défait tout'*) as far as agricultural matters go – so keep an eye on the weather.

(Left) Watermelon ice (recipe, page 129) and a fruit salad. (Right) Limonade à l'ancienne, or old-fashioned lemonade (recipe, page 125) and spiced tea (recipe, page 125) provide welcome refreshment in the summer.

king spicy fi

rrori

Reaso

7. P

wash
Honey Bread
1/4 cup honey instead sugar

FAMILY
FOOD
IDEA

A light Christmas Pudding

90 gms. flour
90 gm bread crumbs (fresh made)
180 gms beef suet chopped fine
180 gms raisins
180 gms currants
120 gms minced apple
150 gms brown sugar
60 gm candied orange peel
2 tsp nutmeg   ¼ tsp ground mace
1 tsp salt   glass brandy, armagnac
                  whiskey or bourbon
3 eggs

Mix well. Very thoroughly.
Grease a pudding bowl. Place a round
of preferred paper which has been greased on
both sides onto the bottom of the bowl.
Fill with the preparation, pressing down
firmly. Cover with another round of
greased, sulferised paper. Sprinkle flour
on a damp tea towel and place over bowl
floured side down. Make a few pleats to

SEPTEMBER

· *In the kitchen* ·

TOMATO COULIS

MAKES 7–10½ PINTS/4–6 LITRES/
4–6 QUARTS

3 tbsp/45 ml/4 tbsp olive oil

2–3 large onions, skinned and sliced

5–6 garlic cloves, skinned

22 lb/10 kg/22 lb tomatoes, thoroughly
washed and coarsely chopped

2–3 celery stalks, sliced

2 whole chillies (optional)

fresh herbs, such as bay leaves, thyme,
basil, fennel, oregano, parsley, to taste

salt and pepper, to taste

Heat the oil in a large saucepan and gently fry the onions and garlic. Add the tomatoes and combine well. Stir in the remaining ingredients. Cook over medium heat until the tomatoes are soft, stirring from time to time to prevent burning.

Put the tomato mixture through the medium grill of a mouli (vegetable mill). Place the pulp in a large bowl and cover with a very fine-weave muslin; place a soup ladle on top of this. The tomato liquid will gradually seep through the cloth into the ladle. As the clear liquid collects, pour it out of the ladle from time to time (to be drunk chilled immediately or frozen and used as a base for soups and stews later) until the purée beneath reaches the desired degree of concentration. Leave overnight and ladle off at least 5–7 pints/3–4 litres/3–4 quarts juice in all.

Place the tomato concentrate in sterilized preserving jars and drizzle a little olive oil on top.

Seal and sterilize for 30 minutes at 200°F/90°C. When cool, check the tops are properly sealed, wipe clean and store.
NOTE: About 13 quarts/15 litres/16 quarts of coulis should see you through the year – unless you give a lot away, which happens all too easily.

RATATOUILLE

MAKES ABOUT 7–8 PINTS/
4–5 LITRES/4–5 QUARTS

2¼ lb/1 kg/2¼ lb aubergines
(eggplants), peeled if desired and diced

salt

olive oil, for frying

2¼ lb/1 kg/2¼ lb mixed green and
yellow courgettes (zucchini and
summer squash), diced

2¼ lb/1 kg/2¼ lb onions, skinned
and sliced

3 green peppers, seeded and sliced

2 chillies seeded and chopped (optional)

11 lb/5 kg/11 lb tomatoes, skinned
and coarsely chopped

4–5 garlic cloves, skinned and crushed

fresh herbs, such as thyme, bay leaves,
basil, oregano, parsley, to taste

salt and pepper, to taste

Place the diced aubergines in a colander and sprinkle liberally with salt. Cover with a plate, place a weight on top, and leave for 1 hour in order to remove the bitter juices.

Rinse and pat dry with absorbent kitchen paper.

Heat the oil in a frying pan and gently fry each vegetable separately, then transfer to a large saucepan. Add the chopped tomatoes, crushed garlic, herbs and seasoning. Cover and simmer for 2 hours.

Place the ratatouille in sterilized preserving jars, drizzle with a little olive oil and add one bay leaf to each jar.

Seal and sterilize the jars for 30 minutes at 200°F/90°C. Suitable for freezing.

SMOKED DUCK

SERVES 4 AS A FIRST COURSE

1 duck, about 4½ lb/2 kg/4½ lb

salt

Prick duck thighs and breast deeply with a sharp fork. Soak in an 80 per cent brine solution (2¾ lb/1.3 kg/5½ cups salt per 1 gallon/4.5 litres/5 quarts water) for 2½ hours. Hang the duck in a cool place for 24 hours to dry. Hot-smoke the duck, using oak shavings, for 2–5 hours, depending on the temperature of the smoker. When cool, slice thinly and serve with curried mayonnaise. Suitable for freezing.
NOTE: Hot-smoking can be done in either a small, portable, box smoker or a large kettle smoker. These are available from kitchen equipment suppliers. Alternatively, a smoker can easily be constructed using house bricks or blocks stacked on top of one another. Form these into a square about 900 mm (3 feet) high. Leave a small draught (draft) hole in the base course, and place a metal dustbin (garbage can) lid on the top. The duck is suspended inside, over smouldering oak shavings.

ROAST PIGEON WITH FOIE GRAS AND MESCLUN SALAD

olive oil, for frying
1 pigeon per person, with giblets
butter
Armagnac, to flambé
½ cup pigeon or chicken stock
1 tbsp/15 ml/1 tbsp port
6 shallots, skinned and chopped
2 tbsp/30 ml/3 tbsp good-quality vinegar
salt and pepper, to taste
Mesclun salad (see Note)
slices of foie gras de canard (see page 94 – also available from speciality shops)

Brown the pigeons in olive oil in a frying pan, adding a little butter to the oil for the last few minutes.

Heat the Armagnac, set alight and pour over the pigeons. Remove pigeons and place in a roasting pan.

Pour off excess fat and deglaze with the pigeon or chicken stock and port.

Roast the pigeons in the oven at 425°F/220°C/mark 7 for about 15 minutes, basting several times with the stock.

Meanwhile, chop the pigeon livers and trim the hearts and gizzards.

Heat the oil in a pan and fry the shallots and giblets. Flambé with Armagnac. Make a vinaigrette using the contents of the pan, olive oil, the vinegar and seasoning.

Toss the *mesclun* salad with half of the vinaigrette and place on a large platter with the slices of *foie gras de canard*. Split the pigeons and serve on the bed of *mesclun* and *foie gras de canard*. Serve the remaining vinaigrette separately.

NOTE: *Mesclun* salad is a mixture of salad vegetables, such as escarole, chicory and treviso, in which the essential ingredients are rocket (arugula) and chervil.

AUBERGINE (EGGPLANT) PURÉE

aubergines (eggplants)
salt and pepper, to taste
lemon juice
olive oil

Grill (broil) the aubergines (eggplants) or bake them at 400°F/200°C/mark 6 for 20 minutes, until soft. Scrape out the flesh and mash with seasoning and a little lemon juice and olive oil. Freeze in convenient-sized containers.

Aubergine purée is incredibly useful through the winter. It can be used in any aubergine casserole and can also be used to prepare all of the following dishes:

AUBERGINE CAVIAR To ¾ pint/450 ml/2 cups purée add a crushed garlic clove and more olive oil and/or lemon juice if needed. Beat well and sprinkle with coriander leaves.

AUBERGINE MEAT BALLS Mix the purée with an equal weight of minced (ground) beef, lamb or veal, 1 egg, 1 chopped, sautéed onion, 1 oz/25 g/¼ cup grated Parmesan cheese and 1 tsp/5 ml/1 tsp ground cumin. Shape into small meatballs, roll in flour and fry. Serve with steamed couscous.

AUBERGINE CRÊPES Add 1 chopped, sautéed onion, 1 egg, 1 tbsp/15 ml/1 tbsp flour and 1 tsp/5 ml/1 tsp baking powder to ¾ pint/450 ml/2 cups purée, and mix together well. Spoon the mixture into hot oil and fry.

JULIE'S MARQUISE AU CHOCOLAT A LA CRÈME ANGLAISE
Rich chocolate dessert with custard sauce

SERVES 8
8 oz/225 g/½ lb cooking (semi-sweet) chocolate, broken into pieces
4 oz/100 g/½ cup butter
3 eggs, separated
3½ oz/90 g/¾ cup icing (confectioners') sugar
FOR THE CUSTARD
1¾ oz/45 g/scant ¼ cup caster (superfine) sugar
4 egg yolks
¾ pint/450 ml/1⅞ cups milk, scalded
½ tsp/5 ml/½ tsp vanilla essence

Melt the chocolate in a double boiler or in a bowl over a pan of hot water.

Work the butter in a bowl until well softened. Add the egg yolks to the butter, one at a time, beating in thoroughly. Add the icing (confectioners') sugar and mix well. Stir in the melted chocolate.

Whisk the egg whites until stiff, and fold into the mixture. Pour into a greased charlotte mould and chill overnight.

The next day, make the custard. Whisk the sugar and egg yolks together until pale and very thick. Add the hot milk in a thin stream, whisking all the time. Cook over a double boiler for 10 minutes, stirring continuously, until thick enough to coat the back of a wooden spoon. Remove from the heat, and immerse the bottom of the pan in cold water. Continue stirring for a minute or two. Strain through a fine sieve or muslin (cheesecloth). Cool.

Turn the dessert out of the mould on to a serving dish and surround with the custard.

BLACKBERRY SORBET (SHERBET)

SERVES 6
l lb/450 g/1 lb blackberries
4 oz/100 g/½ cup sugar
6 fl oz/175 ml/¾ cup water
few leaves of apple mint or rose geranium

Crush the blackberries then pass them through a sieve to remove the pips. Heat the sugar with the water in a pan to make a syrup. Add the apple mint or rose geranium leaves. Leave to cool.

Add the syrup to the purée and place in freezing trays. Freeze for 3 hours, stirring after 2 hours to break up the ice crystals. Alternatively, place in a sorbet (sherbet) maker. Serve sprinkled with mint or geranium leaves.

· In the house ·

Get the house ready for winter. Cut and split wood felled the previous winter. Stack and store in lengths to fit the various stoves and fireplaces. Fill fireside wood baskets.

Repair leaks and faulty shutters. Move back into place all Roman roof tiles which have slipped, and replace broken ones. Remove dead leaves and moss from guttering, and cut back wisteria, roses, Virginia creeper, etc., that have invaded the roof.

Air blankets that have been in mothballs all summer. Put out poison for mice. Sort out cupboards and drawers, putting away summer things. Give the house a thorough cleaning, as in the spring, while the warm weather lasts. Towards the end

of the month, bring in hammocks and garden and pool furniture; clean cushion covers and put away for winter.

· In the garden ·

Think of ordering mixed wildflower seeds in bulk to sow an entire field.

Cut hydrangea blossoms and statice for drying.

OCTOBER

· In the kitchen ·

FOIE GRAS DE CANARD
Duck liver

livers from force-fed ducks
salt and pepper, to taste

To preserve foie gras, wipe the liver, denerve and remove any greenish spots. Season with salt and pepper, and place in sterilized preserving jars. Close and sterilize for 30 minutes at 200°F/90°C for a liver weighing 1 lb/450 g/1 lb. Remove immediately from the sterilizer. Cool, check seals, and store.

The best way to eat foie gras, however, is fresh. Slice the foie into pieces about 1 x 2½ inches/ 6 x 2.5 cm, season lightly and wrap each piece in foil. Heat a frying pan until very hot, add the foil parcels and cook on each side for about 1½ minutes. Serve immediately, in the foil, with fresh bread.

CONFIT DE CANARD
Potted duck

SERVES 4
force-fed ducks (see Method)
rock salt

Fresh *canards gras* (force-fed ducks), which are required for this recipe, are hard to find in many countries outside France. However, if you *can* get them, here is how it is done.

Separate the duck breast and thighs from the carcass, reserving the lump of fat on each side of the entrance to the cavity. Roll the duck portions in rock salt and leave for 24 hours in a cool place.

Render the fat from all remaining parts of the duck, including the skin, by heating in an ungreased pan. Use a fork to press the fat against the bottom of the pan to extract as much fat as possible. Pour off the fat and set aside. Shake the salt from the duck portions.

To prepare the conserve, cook the duck in its rendered fat in a large saucepan on top of the stove, adding the pepper, for about 1 hour or until the juices from the breast run rose-coloured.

Remove and put into sterilized preserving jars – one breast and one thigh per jar. Cover with hot fat, and close. When the fat is cold, sterilize for 30 minutes at 200°F/90°C. Cool, check the seals, and store in a cool place. Can be eaten immediately or kept.

To prepare the duck to be eaten, remove it from its jar, scrape off most of the fat and cook quickly in a very hot oven until the skin is crisp. Slice and serve.

It may also be eaten cold, in which case remove the duck from the jar, scrape off the fat, slice and serve. A breast and a thigh will serve 3 people.

Use the following to make sure that none of the duck carcass is wasted:

DEMOISELLES These are pieces of duck carcass that remain after the *confit* has been removed. They are grilled over the fire or fried in duck fat, then eaten with the fingers.

FRITONS These are crisp, peanut-sized morsels of duck skin, deep-fried in duck fat. They will keep for a week in the refrigerator and can be eaten cold as an accompaniment to drinks or added to green salads.

ALICUIT
Languedoc duck stew

SERVES 6
duck fat
wings, necks, heads and other remaining scraps of 5 force-fed ducks
1 lb/450 g/1 lb carrots, peeled and sliced
2 onions, skinned and sliced
¾ pint/450 ml/2 cups tomato coulis (see page 92)
4 tbsp/60 ml/5 tbsp flour
salt and pepper, to taste

Heat the duck fat in a large frying pan and fry the duck pieces until golden. Transfer to a large casserole.

Gently fry the carrots and onions in the duck fat. Stir in the tomato coulis and simmer for 5 minutes. Add the flour, stirring well.

Pour the vegetable mixture over the duck pieces, cover with boiling water and stir well. Season to taste. Cover and simmer for 2½ hours. Cool, then remove all the duck skin and bones. Serve the dish hot with potatoes, rice or polenta. Suitable for freezing.

ALICE'S JALAPEÑO CHILLI PICKLE

MAKES 10–12 LB/4.5–5.5 KG/ 10–12 LB
¾ lb/350 g/¾ lb tamarind
¾ pints/450 ml/2 cups water
3¼ lb/1.5 kg/3¼ lb garlic, skinned
2¼ lb/1 kg/2¼ lb fresh ginger root
4 oz/100 g/1 cup ground mustard seeds
4 oz/100 g/1 cup ground cumin
¾ pint/450 ml/2 cups malt vinegar
¾ pint/450 ml/2 cups vegetable oil
4½ lb/2 kg/4½ lb jalapeño chillies
1 lb/450 g/2 cups brown sugar

Simmer the tamarind in the water for 20 minutes. Press the pulp through a strainer. Chop the garlic and ginger finely in a food processor or by hand. Make a paste with the ginger, garlic, mustard, cumin and some of the vinegar. Heat a little oil in a large pan and gently fry the paste for 15–20 minutes, stirring continually.

Add the chillies, tamarind, sugar and the remaining vinegar and oil. Bring to the boil, stirring, then simmer for about 15 minutes. Bottle and store. Keeps several years.

NOTE: Salt, lemon juice or grated lemon rind may be added.

JESSIE'S MUFFINS (ENGLISH MUFFINS)

MAKES 20–30
2 tbsp/30 ml/3 tbsp fresh yeast
4 tbsp/60 ml/¼ cup lukewarm water
8 fl oz/250 ml/1 cup milk
2 tbsp/30 ml/2 tbsp sugar
1 tsp/5 ml/1 tsp salt
1 oz/25 g/2 tbsp butter
1 lb/450 g/4 cups plain (all-purpose) flour
1 egg, lightly beaten
cornmeal, for sprinkling

Dissolve the yeast in the lukewarm water and put aside. Scald the milk, then add the sugar, salt and butter. Leave to cool slightly.

When lukewarm, stir in 8 oz/ 225 g/2 cups of the flour, the yeast and egg. Mix thoroughly. Add the remaining flour and combine well.

Turn out the dough on to a lightly floured surface and knead until soft and smooth. Form the dough into a ball and place in a buttered bowl. Butter the surface of the dough and cover with a damp cloth. Leave the dough to rise in a warm

place for 1 hour or until it has doubled in size.

Knock back (punch down) the dough, then leave to rest for 10 minutes. Roll out ¼ inch/5 mm thick on a surface lightly covered with cornmeal. Cut into 3 inch/ 7.5 cm rounds. Sprinkle the tops with cornmeal. Cover with a tea towel and leave to rise until doubled in size, about 45 minutes.

Cook the muffins slowly on an ungreased heavy iron griddle for about 5–6 minutes on each side.

Separate the muffins with a fork, butter and toast. Suitable for freezing.

SALMIS OF PIGEON

SERVES 4–6

4 pigeons, cleaned, livers reserved
duck fat, for frying
3 carrots, peeled and sliced
4 shallots, skinned and chopped
3 tbsp/45 ml/4 tbsp flour
1 bottle strong red wine, such as Madiran
salt and pepper, to taste
2 tbsp/30 ml/3 tbsp Armagnac

Quarter the pigeons. Chop the livers. Heat the duck fat in a frying pan and brown the pigeons. Transfer them to a flameproof casserole.

Add the carrots and shallots to the frying pan and fry until beginning to turn golden. Add the pigeon livers, them immediately add the flour and stir well. Pour in 1 wine glass of the wine, stirring. Pour the contents of the pan over the pigeons. Add enough heated wine to cover the pigeons. Season to taste. Partially cover, then simmer for 2 hours. After 1 hour, add the Armagnac. Serve with triangles of fried bread.

YACOUBI'S TAGINE OF GUINEA FOWL WITH QUINCE

SERVES 4

3 tbsp/45 ml/4 tbsp vegetable oil
1 young guinea fowl, quartered, with skin removed
2 medium red onions, skinned and sliced
1 tbsp/15 ml/1 tbsp ras el hanout (Moroccan spice mixture)
1 tsp/5 ml/1 tsp grated fresh ginger root or ground ginger
1 chilli, seeded and chopped
1 celery stalk, chopped
8–10 cloves
1 tsp/5 ml/1 tsp black pepper
salt
pinch of saffron
1 handful chopped fresh parsley and coriander leaves
6 oz/175 g/1 cup raisins
5 oz/150 g/1 cup blanched almonds
1 tbsp/15 ml/1 tbsp honey
1 tsp/5 ml/1 tsp ground cinnamon
2 quinces, quartered, with peel

Heat the oil in a flameproof casserole and sauté the guinea fowl. Add one of the sliced onions, the ras el hanout, ginger and chilli. Brown thoroughly. Add the remaining sliced onion, the celery, cloves, pepper and saffron. Pour in enough water to just cover, then stir in the parsley and coriander leaves.

Cover and simmer for 25–30 minutes over a low heat. Add the raisins, almonds, honey and cinnamon, stirring well. Place the quinces, skin side up, on top of the fowl. Cover and cook until the quince is soft and the guinea fowl tender. Serve with whole wheat or cracked wheat cooked with apple peel in muslin (cheesecloth), which should be removed before serving.

SUGARED WALNUTS

1 lb/450 g/2 cups sugar
8 fl oz/250 ml/1 cup water
1 lb/450 g/4 cups shelled walnuts

Heat the sugar and water in a saucepan to dissolve sugar. Raise the heat, stirring, until it thickens. Remove from heat and add nuts, stirring continually until completely coated and the syrup has dried. Store in an airtight jar.

ORANGE AND POMEGRANATE SALAD

SERVES 6–8

8 oranges
¾ pint/450 ml/2 cups water
1 lb/450 g/2 cups brown sugar
¼ tsp/1.25 ml/¼ tsp cream of tartar
4 fl oz/120 ml/½ cup orange-flavoured liqueur
seeds of 1 pomegranate

Peel the oranges as thinly as possible, being careful to leave the bitter white pith. Shred the peel finely. Place the peel in a saucepan with the water, sugar and cream of tartar. Bring to a

boil and simmer for 25–30 minutes to make a syrup. Remove from the heat and stir in orange liqueur. Chill.

Remove the white pith from the whole oranges. Arrange the oranges in a serving bowl, cover and chill. To serve, pour the chilled syrup and peel over the oranges. Garnish with the pomegranate seeds.

WALNUT BREAD

SERVES 6

9 oz/250 g/2¼ cups shelled walnuts
6 oz/175 g/1½ cups flour
1½ oz/45 ml/3 tbsp sugar

½ tsp/2.5 ml/½ tsp salt

2 tsp/10 ml/2 tsp baking powder

1 egg

6 fl oz/175 ml/¾ cup milk

Finely chop half the nuts; coarsely chop the rest. Mix nuts in a bowl with the flour, sugar, salt and baking powder. Add the egg and stir in the milk, combining well. Place the mixture in a greased cake tin and leave it in a warm place for 40 minutes, covered with a clean cloth. Bake in the oven at 375°F/190°C/mark 5 for 1 hour. Test with a knife. Turn out of tin; leave to cool. Serve toasted.

· In the house ·

Establish a specific place for outdoor gear, where boots, old jackets, caps, hats, scarves and walking sticks can be kept handy for impromptu walks. Install a bootjack, mudscraper and straw mat in the entrance hall or furnace room to keep mud and dirt out of the house. Update photograph album with all the pictures from the summer holidays. Keep a trunk where exotic old clothes can be saved for the children to dress up in.

· In the garden ·

Plant out spring bulbs. Rake and burn leaves. Bring in pot plants (geraniums, fuchsias, plumbago, oleander, orange and lemon trees and stephanotis) that freeze. Search the hedgerows for autumn bouquets of coloured foliage, berries, rosehips and seed pods such as *Iris foetida*. Pick green tomatoes and wrap in newspaper to ripen.

NOVEMBER

· In the kitchen ·

HUGUETTE'S GARBURE
Vegetable soup

SERVES 6–8

5 pints/3 litres/3 quarts salted water

1 cabbage, green leaves only, thinly sliced

1 lb/450 g/1 lb potatoes, peeled and diced

1 lb/450 g/1lb carrots, peeled and sliced

2 turnips, peeled and sliced

1 lb/450 g/1 lb large white beans, fresh or frozen, or 10 oz/275 g/10 oz dried beans

2 garlic cloves, crushed

confit de canard – 1 breast and 1 thigh (see page 94)

salt and pepper, to taste

If using dried beans, soak them first overnight. Bring the water to the boil in a large saucepan. Add the cabbage leaves, potatoes, carrots, turnips, beans and garlic. Remove as much fat as possible from the *confit* (potted duck) and add to the pan with seasoning to taste. Cover and simmer for 1½ hours. Remove the *confit*, slice and serve with the soup.

DAUBE DE BOEUF
Braised beef stew

SERVES 8–10

4½–5 lbs/2–2.3 kg/4½–5 lb beef, cut into large chunks – use lean beef such as braising steak (rump), with some brisket (short ribs) and a piece of shin (shank)

1¾ pints/1 litre/1 quart strong red wine, such as Madiran

6 carrots, peeled and sliced

6 medium onions, skinned and sliced

3 garlic cloves, skinned and crushed

10 allspice berries

2 bouquets garnis

duck fat, for frying

1 small glass of Armagnac

3 tbsp/45 ml/4 tbsp flour

salt and pepper, to taste

chopped orange rind

Marinate the meat with the wine, carrots, onions, garlic, half of the allspice and the bouquet garni for at least 12 hours. Strain and pat meat dry with absorbent kitchen paper.

Heat the duck fat in a frying pan and brown the meat. Transfer the meat to an earthenware casserole. Brown the carrots, onions and garlic, then transfer to the casserole. Pour the Armagnac over the meat and vegetables. Add the flour to 2 tbsp/30 ml/3 tbsp fat in the frying pan, adding fat if necessary. Stir well and gradually add 1 glass of warmed red wine. Pour over meat and stir. Add enough warmed red wine to cover and a fresh bouquet garni, the remaining allspice, seasoning and a little orange rind.

Cover and cook overnight in the simmering oven of an Aga, in the hot ashes of a fire, or in a conventional oven at 325°F/170°C/mark 3 for at least 4 hours. Remove the meat and vegetables, keeping them warm, and reduce the sauce if necessary. Serve with steamed potatoes.

NOTE: 8 oz/225 g/½ lb pre-soaked prunes can be added before serving. This was a traditional recipe at Marsan, where Victoire grew up.

GIGOT A LA CUILLÈRE

Succulent leg of lamb

SERVES 8–10
1 leg of lamb
1 pig's trotter (foot), split
chicken or veal stock
1 celery stalk
6 onions, skinned and halved
6 carrots, peeled and halved
a few allspice berries
bouquet garni
salt and pepper, to taste
carrots, potatoes, leeks and turnips (to serve)

Place the leg of lamb and pig's trotter (foot) in a large flameproof casserole. Pour in half water and half stock to nearly cover the meat. Add the celery, onions, carrots, allspice, bouquet garni and seasoning to taste. Bring to the boil on top of the stove. Cover and place in the simmering oven of an Aga overnight, or bake in a conventional oven at 225°F/110°C/mark ¼. Alternatively, cook *very* gently for 7–9 hours on top of the stove.

The next morning remove the lamb and keep warm. Remove and discard vegetables and pig's trotter. Reduce the stock to a thick sauce, then remove excess fat.

Serve with the meat and freshly steamed carrots, potatoes, leeks and turnips.

BAKED PEARS IN RED WINE

brown sugar
stick of cinnamon
red wine

Allow 1 large pear or 2 small pears per person. Peel the pears, leaving the stalks on. Arrange in a deep ovenproof dish. Add a stick of cinnamon and 5 oz/150 g/⅔ cup brown sugar per 1 lb/450 g/1 lb pears, and cover with red wine. Leave in the simmering oven of an Aga overnight, or cook in a conventional oven at 300°F/150°C/mark 2 for 1–3 hours, depending on the variety of pears. Turn the pears from time to time.

If necessary, remove the pears and reduce the sauce. Chill the pears and sauce. Serve with crème fraîche.

NOTE: Quartered quinces can also be cooked in the same way.

BRANDY BUTTER

SERVES 4
2 oz/50 g/¼ cup sugar
4 oz/100 g/½ cup butter
1 tbsp/15 ml/1 tbsp Armagnac or Cognac

Cream the sugar and butter together in a bowl. Mix in the Armagnac or Cognac. Cover and chill until needed.

A LIGHT CHRISTMAS PUDDING

SERVES 8–10
3½ oz/90 g/1 cup plain (all-purpose) flour
3½ oz/90 g/1¾ cups fresh breadcrumbs
6 oz/175 g/1 cup beef suet, grated
6 oz/175 g/1 cup raisins
6 oz/175 g/1 cup currants
4½ oz/125 g/1 cup apple, grated
5 oz/150 g/⅝ cup brown sugar
3 oz/75 g/½ cup candied orange peel
½ tsp/2.5 ml/½ tsp grated nutmeg
1 tsp/5 ml/1 tsp salt
¼ tsp/1.25 ml/¼ tsp ground mace
1 glass of Armagnac, brandy, bourbon or Scotch whisky
3 eggs

Mix all the ingredients very thoroughly together in a bowl. Grease one 2¾ pint/1.5 litre/9 cup pudding basin (bowl), or two 1¼ pint/750 ml/3 cup pudding basins.

Place a round of greaseproof paper (waxed paper) on the base of the basin or basins. Fill with the mixture, pressing down firmly. Cover with another round of paper.

Sprinkle flour on a damp cloth and place over the basin, floured side down. Make a few pleats to allow the pudding to swell, and tie with a string around the edge.

Place the basin on a trivet in a large pan filled with hot water to come two-thirds up the sides of the basin.

Cover and simmer for 9 hours, topping up with boiling water as needed.

To store the pudding, once cooked and cooled, remove the cloth and paper. Oil a large piece of greaseproof (waxed) paper and tie it tightly over the basin, oiled side down. Cover with melted wax or paraffin and store in a cool dry place. The pudding will keep for over a year.

To serve, remove the paper. Steam for several hours to heat through. Flambé and serve with brandy butter.

TONY'S BREAD

MAKES TWO LOAVES
1 tbsp/15 ml/1 tbsp dried yeast
½ tsp/2.5 ml/½ tsp honey
2¼ lb/1 kg/2¼ lb wholewheat flour
2 tsp/10 ml/2 tsp salt
8 fl oz/250 ml/1 cup natural (plain) yogurt

Stir the yeast and honey into a little warm water, and leave until frothy.

Sift the flour and salt into a mixing bowl and make a well in the centre. Add the yeast mixture and the natural (plain) yogurt, with enough warm water to work the mixture into an elastic, smooth dough.

Divide the dough in half and place in two greased loaf tins. Cover with a clean cloth and allow to rise for 2 hours in a warm place until the dough has doubled in size.

Bake the loaves in the oven at 325°F/170°C/mark 3 for 30 minutes to 1 hour or until the loaves sound hollow when tapped on the bottom with the knuckles.

· In the house ·

Bleed (purge) radiators and check insulation and drafts. Wrap all exposed water pipes with straw and plastic. Order Christmas presents and send off packages abroad. Make the rounds of the local junkshops (plentiful in Gascony) in search of gifts. Begin to wrap presents. Help the children with the pomanders of cloves and oranges they make for friends and family.

· In the garden ·

Plant garlic, shallots, local sweet spring onion, artichokes, strawberries, fruit trees, roses, biennials and perennials (including the Christmas and Lenten Rose). Sow broad (fava) beans, peas, and sweet peas. Prune spring-blooming trees. Lift dahlias. Add compost to unoccupied parts of vegetable garden in anticipation of spring planting. Clear lilacs of suckers, planting them elsewhere. Put straw over or around all plants which can be damaged by a hard freeze, such as bay laurels, mimosas, olives, certain roses (Mermaid), pomegranates, cistus, artichokes.

Ivy, which at this time of year is laden with small black and green berries, makes an attractive arrangement (though some people think this a plant of ill omen). Bouquets can be made with dried flowers and seed heads, such as those of cow parsley, dock and thistle.

DECEMBER

· *In the kitchen* ·

PATRICK'S OIE DE GUINÉE RÔTIE

Roast goose

SERVES 6
young goose, about 7 lb/3.2 kg/7 lb
salt and pepper

Place goose in a roasting tin and season with salt and pepper. Roast in the oven at 425°F/220°C/mark 7 for 30 minutes, then reduce the heat to 325°F/170°C/mark 3 and roast for a further 1½ hours, until golden brown, basting every 15 minutes with its own juices. Remove excess fat from the juices before serving.

POMMES DAUPHINES

Dauphine potatoes

SERVES 8–10
1½ lb/700 g/1½ lb potatoes, peeled
oil, for deep frying
FOR THE CHOUX PASTE
8 fl oz/250 ml/1 cup water
4 tbsp/60 ml/⅓ cup peanut oil
coarse salt, to taste
4½ oz/115 g/1 cup plus 2 tbsp flour
3–4 eggs
white pepper
grated nutmeg

Steam or boil the potatoes until tender. Drain and purée in a mouli (vegetable mill) or blender. Dry them if necessary in an open oven to remove any excess moisture.

Heat the water, oil and salt together in a saucepan. As soon as it begins to boil, remove from the heat and add the flour, beating vigorously until it forms a smooth batter. Cool a little, then add the eggs, one at a time. The mixture will form a greasy ball that no longer sticks to the sides of the pan.

Add the potato purée to the choux paste, a spoonful at a time, until it is all incorporated into the mixture. Season with salt, pepper and nutmeg. Heat oil in a deep fat fryer. With a spoon, form the mixture into little balls and quickly drop them into the hot oil. When cooked, keep warm while frying the remainder.

CORN BREAD

MAKES TWO 8 INCH/20 CM SQUARE LOAVES
6 oz/175 g/1½ cups plain (all-purpose) flour
8 oz/225 g/1½ cups cornmeal
6 tsp/30 ml/6 tsp baking powder
1½ tsp/7.5 ml/1½ tsp salt
4 tbsp/60 ml/⅓ cup sugar
12 fl oz/350 ml/1½ cups milk
2 eggs, beaten
5 tbsp/75 ml/6 tbsp melted butter

Mix the flour, cornmeal, baking powder, salt and sugar in a bowl and make a well in the centre. Mix in the milk, eggs and melted butter. Grease two 8 inch/20 cm square pans, and heat in the oven. Transfer the mixture to the pans. Bake in the oven at 425°F/220°C/mark 7 for 25 minutes.

MILSTER'S CORN BREAD STUFFING FOR TURKEY

two 8 inch/20 cm loaves corn bread (see this page)
oil, for frying
1 large onion, skinned and chopped
2 green peppers, seeded and chopped
2 celery stalks, chopped
bunch of parsley, chopped
6 oz/175 g/1½ cups pecans, chopped
salt and pepper, to taste
1 tbsp/15 ml/1 tbsp brown sugar
½ tsp/2.5 ml/½ tsp chopped fresh sage
½ tsp/2.5 ml/½ tsp chopped fresh thyme
½ tsp/2.5 ml/½ tsp chopped fresh oregano
2 eggs
small glass of sherry
FOR THE STOCK
turkey giblets and neck
1 carrot, peeled and halved
1 onion, skinned and halved
1 bouquet garni
salt and pepper, to taste

Allow the corn bread to cool, then crumble into a large bowl. To make the stock, place the turkey giblets, neck, carrot, onion, bouquet garni and seasoning in a saucepan and simmer for 1 hour. Strain the stock, then chop the giblet meat.

Heat the oil in a pan and lightly sauté the onion, green

peppers, and celery. Add to the corn bread with the parsley, pecans, seasoning, brown sugar, sage, thyme, oregano, chopped giblets, eggs, sherry and enough stock from the giblets to moisten. Mix well. Use to stuff the turkey *just* before roasting.

AMBROSIA

SERVES 8
4–5 large navel oranges
1 medium pineapple
1 small coconut
brown sugar, to taste
juice of 2 oranges
juice of 1 lemon
dash of Armagnac

Peel the navel oranges, removing all white pith and membrane. Slice and cut into chunks. Peel and cut the pineapple into chunks. Crack the coconut and grate the flesh, reserving the milk. Sprinkle the fruit mixture with brown sugar, the orange and lemon juice, half the coconut milk and a dash of Armagnac. Mix well. Place in a crystal bowl and chill.

SAVANNAH AND JACK'S TRUFFES AU CHOCOLAT
Chocolate truffles

MAKES 12–20
1 lb/450 g/1 lb bitter chocolate, broken into pieces
2 tbsp/30 ml/3 tbsp water
2 tbsp/30 ml/3 tbsp sugar
6 oz/175 g/³⁄₄ cup butter
2 egg yolks
cocoa powder or crushed nuts, to coat

Melt the chocolate with the water, sugar and butter in the top of a double boiler, or in a bowl over a pan of hot water. Stir well, remove from the heat and allow to cool a little. When just warm, beat in the egg yolks. Chill in the refrigerator for about 5 hours.

Mould the chocolate mixture into small balls. Roll in the cocoa powder or crushed nuts. Keep chilled.

NOTE: Truffles may be flavoured with 2 tbsp/30 ml/3 tbsp Armagnac, brandy, rum or other alcohol when the egg yolks are added.

CREOLE SAUSAGE

MAKES ABOUT 40 SAUSAGEMEAT BALLS
2 lb/900 g/2 lb unseasoned sausagemeat
1 tbsp/15 ml/1 tbsp salt
FOR THE CREOLE SEASONING
8 bay leaves
1 tsp/5 ml/1 tsp fresh thyme
1 tsp/5 ml/1 tsp fresh oregano
1 tsp/5 ml/1 tsp fresh sage
1 tsp/5 ml/1 tsp black peppercorns
1 tsp/5 ml/1 tsp coriander seeds
4 dried chillies, or to taste
20 allspice berries

For the Creole seasoning, pulverize the seasoning ingredients in an electric coffee grinder.

For the sausagemeat, mix the unseasoned sausagemeat, salt and 2 tbsp/30 ml/3 tbsp of the Creole seasoning together in a ball. Roll into a sausage shape, wrap in foil and refrigerate or freeze until needed.

For the sausagemeat balls, form the sausage into small balls and fry until they are cooked through. They can be eaten on their own, or wrapped in croissant or puff pastry dough and baked. Serve hot.

ÎLE FLOTTANTE
Floating island

SERVES 8–10
1³⁄₄ pints/1 litre/4¹⁄₂ cups milk, plus extra for poaching
5 oz/150 g/²⁄₃ cup sugar
2 split vanilla pods (beans)
10 eggs, separated
1 tbsp/15 ml/1 tbsp cornflour (cornstarch)
6 tbsp/90 ml/7 tbsp sugar, for the caramel

Place the milk, sugar and vanilla in a saucepan and bring to the boil. Remove from heat and take out the vanilla pods. Beat the egg yolks with the cornflour (cornstarch) in a bowl. Pour the warm milk slowly into the egg mixture, stirring constantly with a wooden spoon. Return to a low heat (do not allow to boil or the eggs will curdle), and stir until the custard thickens enough to coat the back of the spoon. Remove from heat and pour the custard through a fine sieve into a large serving dish.

Whisk the whites with a pinch of salt until stiff. Poach spoonfuls of the egg whites, the size of an egg, in a pan of simmering milk for 1 minute. Turn them over gently and poach for another minute. Drain and place on top of the custard.

Just before serving make the caramel. Place the sugar and 1 tbsp/15 ml/1 tbsp cold water in a heavy-based saucepan. Place over a medium heat and turn the pan until the caramel turns golden. Place the pan in cold water. Allow to cool slightly, then spin the caramel over the egg whites with a wooden spoon.

GRANITÉ DE POMMES VERTES A LA FINE BLANCHE
Apple ice with Fine Blanche

crisp green apples, such as 'Granny Smith' (allow ½ apple per person)
sugar
Fine Blanche (an unaged blend of Armagnac)

Peel and chop apples, then freeze. Purée in a food processor or blender, adding 1 tsp/ 5 ml/1 tsp sugar per apple. Serve the apple ice in small stemmed glasses with Fine Blanche poured on top.

ANTHONY'S MINCEMEAT

ENOUGH FOR 12–16 SMALL PIES
1 lb/450 g/1 lb apples
6 oz/175 g/1 cup shredded beef suet
4 oz/100 g/⅔ cup raisins
4 oz/100 g/⅔ cup currants
4 oz/100 g/⅔ cup sultanas (golden raisins)
4 oz/100 g/1 cup grated orange and lemon rind (fresh or candied)
juice of ½ lemon
1 tsp/5 ml/1 tsp ground cinnamon
pinch of ground ginger
¼ tsp/1.25 ml/¼ tsp grated nutmeg
12 oz/350 g/1½ cups brown sugar
1 tsp/5 ml/1 tsp salt
3 tbsp/45 ml/¼ cup Armagnac
3 tbsp/45 ml/¼ cup sherry

Mix all the ingredients in a food processor; or mince fruit by hand and mix all the ingredients in a large bowl. Pack well in airtight jars. Allow to mature for several weeks before using as a filling for shortcrust pastry. Can be kept for a year or so.

BRÛLOT

1 bottle of Armagnac
20 sugar cubes

This ancient local brew is dynamite, only to be attempted by those determined to '*prendre une cuite*' – i.e. get very drunk very quickly. Innocent newcomers to Gascony are often trapped into hilarious brûlot sessions, which invariably end with the hangover of a lifetime. Brûlot is delicious, but no one in their right mind will take more than one glass of it at a sitting.

Pour the Armagnac into a large saucepan and bring to boiling point, mixing in the sugar cubes. Light with a match and ladle repeatedly as the Armagnac flares. Serve piping hot in coffee cups when the flame dies down.

· In the house ·

Polish all the silver and check all table linen. Have in reserve Christmas wrapping paper, ribbon, cards, cellophane tape, an assortment of candles and paper napkins, a few small presents wrapped and ready for last-minute guests, and plenty of wine and champagne.

BAY LEAF WREATH

Cut a length of chicken wire about 3 feet/90 cm long and 1 foot/30 cm wide. Bend the two ends together and crumple it into a circular shape. Fill spaces in wire with sprigs and small branches of bay, all facing in the same direction, until the wire is completely hidden. Use small wires to shape if necessary. Add ornaments and a bow.

· In the garden ·
BIRDS' CHRISTMAS TREE

Choose an appropriate shrub or small tree that can be seen from the house so you can watch the birds discover it. Decorate it with garlands of popcorn, rosehips and red, edible berries such as cranberries. Hang on it slices of apple and tangerine and suet balls rolled in grain and tied with coloured ribbons.

JANUARY

· In the kitchen ·

TARTE A L'OIGNON
Onion pie

SERVES 4–6
FOR THE PASTRY
7 oz/200 g/1⅔ cups plain (all-purpose) flour
¼ tsp/1.25 ml/¼ tsp salt
4 oz/100 g/1 cup Cheddar cheese, grated
4 oz/100 g/½ cup butter or margarine
FOR THE FILLING
olive oil, for frying
5 large onions, skinned and thinly sliced
5 anchovy fillets, chopped
small black olives
anchovy fillets
ground black pepper
fresh thyme
grated Parmesan cheese

For the pastry, sift the flour and salt into a bowl. Work in the grated cheese. Rub in the butter or margarine until the mixture resembles fine breadcrumbs. Add about 3 tbsp/45 ml/¼ cup iced water and work to a dough. Roll out and use to line a pie dish.

For the filling, heat the oil in a pan and sweat the onions and anchovy fillets over a very low heat. When the onions are very soft, spread evenly over the pastry case (pie crust). Decorate with the black olives and more anchovy fillets. Sprinkle with black pepper, thyme and grated Parmesan. Bake in the oven at 325°F/170°C/mark 3 for about 30 minutes.

BÉCASSE A LA FICELLE

Woodcock Gascon-style

woodcock (allow one per person)
duck fat
bread (allow one slice per person)
foie gras
salt and pepper, to taste
Armagnac

If you're lucky enough to find yourself in possession of a brace or so of woodcock, try this classic Gascon method of preparing them.

Pluck the woodcock, but do not remove their insides. Rub with duck fat. Suspend them, by a string tied around their beaks, in front of a good wood fire with plenty of hot coals. Beneath each bird, on a grid below, place a slice of toasted bread spread with fresh foie gras. Twist the strings by which the woodcock are suspended and allow them to cook for about 30–45 minutes as the strings slowly unwind. Rewind when necessary.

Just before serving, place the slice of toast in the oven for a few minutes, to ensure that the woodcock drippings are thoroughly cooked. Place the woodcock on the toast, season with salt and pepper, flambé with Armagnac and serve.

SPICY SHEPHERD'S PIE

SERVES 6–8
FOR THE TOPPING
3 lb/1.4 kg/3 lb potatoes
1 onion, skinned and sliced
salt and white pepper, to taste
1 bay leaf
1 tbsp/15 ml/1 tbsp brown sugar
4 oz/100 g/½ cup butter
12 fl oz/375 ml/1½ cups milk, warmed
FOR THE FILLING
duck fat or vegetable oil, for frying
2 onions, skinned and chopped
2 garlic cloves, skinned and chopped
1 chilli, seeded and chopped
2 lb/900 g/2 lb minced (ground) beef
1 tsp/5 ml/1 tsp chopped fresh thyme
2 tsp/10 ml/2 tsp chopped fresh dill
2 tsp/10 ml/2 tsp ground cumin
½ tsp/2.5 ml/½ tsp fennel seeds
1 tsp/5 ml/1 tsp chilli seasoning
pinch of rosemary, oregano, ground ginger and ground coriander
5 oz/150 g/1 cup blanched almonds, chopped
6 oz/175 g/1 cup raisins
flaked (slivered) almonds, for sprinkling
1 egg, beaten
butter
grated Parmesan cheese

For the topping, place the potatoes, onion, salt to taste and bay leaf in a saucepan of boiling water and cook until tender. Pass through a vegetable mill, or mash, then stir in the sugar, butter, milk and seasoning until fluffy and fairly runny.

For the filling, heat the duck fat or vegetable oil in a pan and sauté the onion, garlic and chilli. Add the meat and seasonings and continue to sauté for about 15 minutes. Add the almonds and raisins. Place the meat mixture in the base of an ovenproof dish. Add the potato purée and sprinkle with flaked (slivered) almonds. Brush with beaten egg, dot with slices of butter and top with Parmesan. Bake in the oven at 400°F/200°C/mark 6 until the top is brown and sizzling.

NOTE: The seasonings for the meat filling can be altered according to personal taste but the cumin and dill are essential.

BAKED SMOKED HAM

1 ham (see Method)
cider
cloves
8 fl oz/250 ml/1 cup maple syrup
2 tsp/10 ml/2 tsp dry mustard
½ tsp/2.5 ml/½ tsp ground cloves

Choose a ham which has been lightly salted, hung and cold-smoked, such as Virginia or York ham.

Soak the ham overnight in enough cold water to cover. Drain the ham then place in a saucepan, and cover with half cold water and half cider. Bring to the boil and simmer for 2 hours, regardless of the weight of the ham.

Remove from the heat and allow the ham to cool in the cooking liquid.

Cut off the rind. Score the fat, and stud with cloves. Make a glaze with the maple syrup, mustard and cloves, and brush the ham with this mixture. Bake in the oven at 325°F/170°C/mark 3 for 30 minutes per pound, increasing the heat to 425°F/220°C/mark 7 for the last 45 minutes, and basting from time to time.

GALETTE DE POMMES DE TERRE
Gascon fried potato pancake

SERVES 4
1½ lb/700 g/1½ lb potatoes
4 tbsp/60 ml/⅓ cup duck fat
salt and pepper, to taste
garlic, chopped
fresh parsley, chopped

Slice potatoes very thinly. Heat the duck fat in a large frying pan, add a layer of sliced potatoes and season generously. Add another layer of potatoes. Season again, then cook for 3 minutes over a fairly high heat. Reduce the heat to medium to cook the potatoes. When the bottom is brown and crispy, turn over (sliding a plate underneath if necessary, to hold the pancake together) and brown on the other side. Transfer to a large flat serving dish, and sprinkle chopped garlic and parsley over the potato pancake.

POLENTA SOUFFLÉ

SERVES 10–12
3 quarts/3.4 litres/4 quarts water
1 lb/450 g/1 lb polenta or cornmeal
3–4 garlic cloves, crushed
6 oz/175 g/1½ cups Cheddar or Gruyère cheese, grated
3 oz/75 g/¾ cup grated Parmesan cheese
4 oz/100 g/½ cup butter
salt and pepper, to taste
5 egg yolks
7 egg whites

Bring the water to the boil, and add the polenta gradually in a very thin stream, stirring constantly. Simmer very gently, stirring frequently, for about 20 minutes until cooked. Add the garlic, cheeses, butter and seasoning. Remove from the heat and stir in the egg yolks one at a time. Whisk the egg whites until stiff and fold one half into the polenta mixture very thoroughly. Add other half very gently. Pour into a buttered medium-deep ovenproof dish. Bake in the oven at 350°F/180°C/mark 4 for 45 minutes.

HENRY'S CONFITURE D'OIGNONS
Sweet onion pickle

10 lb/4.5 kg/10 lb onions, skinned and very thinly sliced
6 lbs/2.7 kg/6 lb brown sugar
2¾ pints/1.5 litres/6½ cups malt or cider vinegar
24 cloves
3–4 dried chillies, to taste
salt and pepper, to taste

Place all the ingredients in a large saucepan and simmer very slowly for 2½ hours. Bottle in sterilized jars.

· In the house ·

Check all household linen and mend as necessary. Rebind frayed towels or make into oven gloves or flannels (wash cloths) if unmendable. Cut sheets worn in the middle in two and sew together again by the outside edges. Sew missing buttons on pillow cases.

Lay out rugs and blankets in dry powdery snow, which is full of ammonia and is a natural cleaner.

NATHALIE'S RABBIT-SKIN GLUE PAINT

Make this paint with rabbit-skin glue, powdered natural pigment and whitening, such as Blanc d'Espagne, Meudon or Troyes. All the ingredients are to be found in a well-stocked art supply shop.

This technique has several advantages. Colours using natural pigments are far more intense and subtle than those of conventional paint. Also, the thickness of the paint with its slightly irregular surface confers a sculptural quality on the most mundane piece of furniture.

In a bain marie dissolve 3½–4 oz/100–125 g/3½–4 oz rabbit-skin glue in 1¾ pints/1 litre/4¼ cups of water. Mix with a wooden spoon until smooth. Add 2¼ lb/1 kg/2¼ lb whitening and stir until well blended. Mix a little pigment separately with cold water. Stir into the original mixture till you have obtained the desired colour. A little pigment goes quite a long way so test the colour on paper first. It dries quickly and slightly paler. The paint must remain in the bain marie (with hot water being added as necessary) while it is being used. It will keep for eight days and can be reheated. Apply three coats of paint, the third quite roughly. When completely dry, sand with glasspaper (very fine sandpaper) lightly and quickly till the powder falls and the paint shines. Clean with a dust cloth, then wax. Apply several coats of liquid wax if you want to be able to wash off fingerprints.

BABA'S FURNITURE REVIVER

Make furniture reviver in the following proportions: 2 parts malt vinegar, 2 parts methylated spirits, 2 parts pure turpentine, 1 part boiled linseed oil. Pour all ingredients into a sealable bottle. Always shake thoroughly before use – the liquid should have a milky consistency.

Apply with a small pad of cotton wool (cotton), rubbing off the dirt. Wipe off residue with a soft rag. Apply to all polished furniture once a year; wax afterwards.

BEESWAX FURNITURE POLISH

Fill a jam jar one-quarter full with small pieces of real beeswax. Add pure turpentine to approximately half full. Place the jar in a saucepan of cold water and bring to the boil. Simmer until the wax has completely melted. Remove from the water and cool. Seal the top.

To use, put a small amount of the mixture on a cotton rag. Rub into the grain of the furniture, until the surface is covered.

Allow to dry for a couple of hours, then rub off with a soft cloth. Always finish off with a cloth moving in the direction of the grain. Do not put anything on the surface until the next day. Rub off any residue. Apply once a year.

· In the garden ·

If it is not too wet or cold, roses and shrubs can be transplanted. Vines, fruit trees, roses, wisteria and hedges may be pruned or trimmed. Order summer bulbs such as lilies, begonias and dahlias. Poppies and larkspur can be sown out-of-doors. Indoors, sow seeds of scented tobacco and other plants in flats, then keep them in a warm, sunny place, until they are planted out in spring.

FEBRUARY

· In the kitchen ·

POULE AU POT
Chicken in the pot

SERVES 8
1 large hen
2 carrots, peeled
1 turnip, peeled
1 whole leek, washed and trimmed
1 unskinned onion, stuck with a few cloves
3 bay leaves
sprig of thyme
salt and pepper, to taste
large cabbage leaves

FOR THE STUFFING
1 onion, skinned
1 garlic clove, skinned
bunch of parsley
2 leeks, with tender green part
2 slices cured ham
chicken liver, heart and gizzard
3 dried cep mushrooms, soaked (optional)
3 slices of stale bread, crusts removed, soaked in milk
12 oz/350 g/³/₄ lb minced (ground) pork
12 oz/350 g/³/₄ lb minced (ground) veal
1 tsp/5 ml/1 tsp dill
1 tsp/5 ml/1 tsp ground cumin
salt and pepper, to taste
2 eggs
FOR THE RICE
2 tbsp/30 ml/2 tbsp chicken fat, skimmed from stock
1 onion, skinned and chopped
14 oz/400 g/2 cups long grain rice
1³/₄ pints/1 litre/1 quart hot chicken stock
FOR THE VEGETABLES
1 lb/450 g/1 lb carrots, peeled and sliced
1 lb/450 g/1 lb turnips, peeled and sliced
1 lb/450 g/1 lb leeks, trimmed, washed and sliced
FOR THE SAUCE
3 tbsp/45 ml/4 tbsp butter
3 tbsp/45 ml/4 tbsp flour
1 pint/600 ml/2¹/₂ cups hot chicken stock
8 fl oz/250 ml/1 cup crème fraîche or cream
2 egg yolks
salt and white pepper, to taste
juice of 1 lemon

For the stuffing, chop the onion, garlic, parsley, leeks, ham, giblet meat, cep mushrooms and

105

bread together in a food processor. Add to the pork and veal and mix well. Stir in the dill, cumin, seasoning and eggs, combining well.

Fill the cavity of the chicken with stuffing and sew up. Place in a large cooking pot. Add the carrots, turnip, whole leek, onion stuck with cloves, bay leaves, thyme and seasoning. Cover with cold water. Bring to the boil, cover and simmer for at least 4 hours or until tender. Alternatively, place overnight in the simmering oven of an Aga.

When cooked, remove the chicken and keep warm. Ladle off sufficient stock to cook the rice, vegetables and cabbage parcels.

For the rice, heat the chicken fat in a flameproof casserole (or Dutch oven) and fry the onion. Add the rice and sauté until transparent. Stir in the hot stock. Cover and cook in the oven at 325°F/170°C/mark 3 for 25 minutes or until the rice is tender.

For the parcels, choose large, green, unblemished outside leaves of the cabbage. Drop into a saucepan of hot chicken stock for 1–2 minutes to soften. Remove and drain. Place a few tablespoons of stuffing in each leaf. Fold the edges over and tie up with kitchen string as you would a parcel. Poach the parcels in the simmering chicken stock for about 15–20 minutes. Cook the vegetables in the stock along with cabbage parcels until just tender.

For the sauce, melt the butter in a pan and add the flour. Stir well and gradually pour in the hot chicken stock, stirring until smooth. In a bowl, combine the crème fraîche and egg yolks. Stir a cup of the hot sauce into the egg yolk mixture. Then add this mixture to the remaining sauce in the pan and stir well. Add salt, if necessary, and white pepper. Just before serving, stir in the lemon juice. Do not allow to boil.

To serve, remove the skin from the chicken. Surround with the vegetables and cabbage parcels. Pour a little sauce over the chicken. Serve the rice and remaining sauce separately.

CASSOULET

Languedoc bean stew

SERVES 10
3 lb/1.4 kg/3 lb frozen or 2 lbs/900 g/ 2 lb dried white beans, such as haricot (navy) or butter (lima) beans
1 bay leaf
1 strip of pig skin, cut in 2 inch/5 cm pieces
4 pieces confit de canard (see page 94 – also available from speciality shops)
10 fresh sausages, cut in two
1 lb/450 g/1 lb unsmoked bacon, cut into large cubes
5–6 large carrots, peeled and sliced
2 large onions, skinned and chopped
3/4 pint/450 ml/2 cups tomato coulis (see page 92)
3 tbsp/45 ml/4 tbsp flour
salt and pepper, to taste

If using dried beans, soak them overnight in cold water. Cook the beans in boiling salted water with the bay leaf and pig skin. If the beans rise to the surface, remove from the heat and wait until they sink. Cook until soft. Drain.

Melt the fat off the *confit de canard* in a pan; remove to a large earthenware casserole. In the duck fat remaining in the pan, fry the sausages and transfer to the casserole. Fry the bacon in the pan and transfer to the casserole. Sauté the carrots in the pan and, after a few minutes, add the onions and continue cooking for 3–4 minutes. Add the tomato coulis and cook for 5 minutes. Sprinkle over the flour and stir very well. Add the vegetable and tomato mixture to the casserole with the beans. Season to taste. Cover with boiling water, stir well and cover the casserole.

Cook in the oven at 375°F/ 190°C/mark 5 for 2 hours. Remove the lid and continue to cook for 15 minutes or until a crust forms on the top.

BLACK BEAN SOUP

SERVES 4
duck fat or vegetable oil, for frying
1 onion, skinned and chopped
2 celery stalks, chopped
1 garlic clove, skinned and chopped
1½ lb/700 g/4 cups frozen or 1 lb/450 g/2½ cups dried black beans
2 bay leaves
1 whole chilli (optional)
1 ham bone
salt and pepper
3½ pints/2 litres/2 quarts boiling water
hard-boiled egg slices, to garnish
sherry
lemon juice

Heat the duck fat or vegetable oil and sauté the onion, celery and garlic. Add fresh or frozen beans, or dried beans that have been soaked overnight, the bay leaves, chilli, ham bone, seasoning and boiling water. Cover and simmer for 1 hour, then uncover and simmer for 1 hour (a little longer if the beans are dried), adding water if necessary. Remove the bay leaf, chilli and ham bone. Cool slightly, then purée in a blender or food processor. Reheat and serve, garnished with sliced hard-boiled egg. Add a tot of sherry to each bowl and a squeeze of lemon juice.

PÂTÉ

pork liver and belly
lean pork left over after making sausages
5 shallots
pulp remaining from 6 garlic cloves chopped and pressed through sieve (when making dried sausage – see below)
salt and pepper, to taste
ground allspice

Pass the meat through the fine blade of a mincer with the shallots and the garlic pulp. Season the meat with salt and pepper and allspice. Place in jars, seal and sterilize at 200°F/90°C for 3 hours.

SAUCISSON
Dried sausages

MAKES 11 LB/5 KG/11 LB
11 lb/5 kg/11 lb lean pork, such as shoulder
10 tsp/50 ml/10 tsp salt
5 tsp/25 ml/5 tsp pepper
nutmeg or allspice, to taste
glass of red wine
6 garlic cloves, chopped
crushed peppercorns

Put the meat through the medium cutter of a mincer (grinder). Add the salt, pepper, nutmeg or allspice, and wine. Press the chopped garlic through a fine cloth, and add the juice to the meat mixture. (The pulp can be used for making

pâté – see left.) Mix well, then feed into medium-sized casings. Tie in lengths of about 8 inches/20 cm and roll in crushed peppercorns. Hang for 30–40 days in a cool, dry place. When sufficiently dry, roll the sausages in finely powdered wood ash. Serve with fresh country bread and butter.

TANGERINE JAM

MAKES ABOUT 8 LB/3.6 KG/8 LB
5 lb/2.3 kg/5 lb clementines or tangerines, organically grown
2 lemons
4 lbs/1.8 kg/4 lb sugar

Wash and dry the clementines or tangerines and lemons. Cut them into very thin slices (this can be done in a food processor). Put in a porcelain or terracotta bowl and cover with water. Leave for 12 hours.

The next day, put the fruit and water into a preserving pan and cook over a medium heat for 25 minutes. Pour back into the bowl and leave for 24 hours.

On the third day, add the sugar and return to the preserving pan. Simmer for 1 hour. Pot and seal. Sterilize at 212°F/100°C for 25 minutes.

ORANGE MARMALADE

MAKES ABOUT 12 LB/5.4 KG/12 LB
2 lb/900 g/2 lb Seville oranges, organically grown
2½ lb/1.1 kg/2½ lb sweet oranges
2 lemons
4 pints/2.3 litres/2½ quarts water
8½ lb/3.9 kg/8½ lb brown sugar
glass of Armagnac or whisky (optional)

Wash the oranges and lemons well. Cut in half and squeeze the juice. Remove the pips from the pulp and tie in muslin (cheesecloth). Slice the peel thinly and place with juice, pulp, pips and water in a preserving pan. Place a piece of greaseproof (waxed) paper over the surface of the liquid, and cover tightly. Leave overnight in the simmering oven of an Aga, or simmer over a low heat for 2 hours then leave until the next day.

The next morning, remove the paper from the surface, warm the sugar, and add to the pan. Boil until setting point is reached. If you like, add a glass of Armagnac or whisky. Remove the bag of pips and squeeze. Allow the marmalade to cool for 30 minutes. Stir well and pot in sterilized jars.

WINTER RADISH AND ANCHOVY SALAD

SERVES 4–6 AS A FIRST COURSE
24 fresh anchovies, cleaned and filleted
sea salt
juice of 1 lemon
2 tbsp/30 ml/3 tbsp olive oil
4 large, red, carrot-shaped radishes, very thinly sliced
freshly ground pepper
coriander leaves, to garnish

Sprinkle the anchovies with sea salt and leave to drain in a colander for 30 minutes. Rinse and drain. Marinate in the lemon juice and 1 tbsp/15 ml/1 tbsp of the olive oil for 1–2 hours. Mix the radishes with the anchovies. Add the remaining olive oil and pepper. Garnish with coriander leaves.

VICTOIRE'S UNCLE ANDRÉ DE VILMORIN'S RED CABBAGE SALAD

SERVES 6
1 red cabbage
fine sea salt
1 tbsp/15 ml/1 tbsp peppercorns
3–4 bay leaves, crumbled
3 tbsp/45 ml/4 tbsp vinegar
3 tbsp/45 ml/4 tbsp water
walnut oil

Place the cabbage in a bowl, sprinkle with fine sea salt and leave to macerate for 2 days in the refrigerator. Drain and place in a large bowl with the peppercorns, bay leaves, vinegar and water. Macerate for another 24 hours. Remove the peppercorns and bay leaves. Drain. Season with walnut oil.

· *In the house* ·

Continue with the spring cleaning started in January. Rearrange the books in the library, cleaning leather bindings with saddle soap. Make the rounds of empty rooms and inspect for signs of mice – which make nests in mattresses, drawers, sofas and chairs.

The following techniques for cleaning metals came from Eugène, the butler at the Montesquious' château at Marsan. COPPER: Rub with half a lemon covered in scouring powder. Wipe and shine with a woollen cloth. PEWTER: Rub pewter with chopped outer leaves of a raw cabbage; rinse with clean water and rub again with the green part of a leek; rinse again and dry with an old linen cloth. SILVER: Make a paste with whitening such as blanc d'Espagne and methylated spirits, and smear on silver. Remove with a soft brush when dry, and polish with a soft cloth. Tarnished silver cutlery can be brightened by rubbing with turning alcohol. Egg-darkened silver can be cleaned by soaking in water in which potatoes have been boiled.

To remove from furniture water stains that are still fresh, wipe immediately and then wax before the mark is dry. If the surface has been well cared for, brushing carefully with a natural-fibre scrubbing brush will make the mark disappear. Difficult marks can be removed by rubbing with a cloth dipped in hot milk, followed by a little oil on a wool cloth. Wax the furniture as usual.

· *In the garden* ·

Continue planting fruit trees, roses and shrubs if the weather allows. Prune, fertilize and graft fruit trees; treat with Bordeaux mixture.

Take cuttings from fuchsias. Plant out asparagus, shallots, strawberries, and globe and Jerusalem artichokes.

See to espaliered trees now, before they are in bud.

Work well-rotted compost and manure into the vegetable garden, and prepare the ground for planting potatoes and sowing in March. Hoe around broad beans and peas. Work the ground around rose bushes, and fertilize. Plant thyme and lily of the valley.

Sow lawns and treat existing lawn for moss and lichens.

MARCH

· *In the kitchen* ·

SERGE'S DANDELION SALAD

dandelion leaves (see method)
3 tbsp/45 ml/4 tbsp butter
1 tbsp/15 ml/1 tbsp vinegar
salt and pepper, to taste

Dandelions are best eaten before the plant has begun to flower. The tenderest leaves are those of the crown that are partly under the surface of the ground and therefore slightly blanched. Cut the plants off with part of the root attached so that the leaves will hold together. Discard the tougher outer leaves from the dandelions. Wash the dandelions four times, then detach from the root and wash once more. Dry and set aside.

Melt the butter in a deep frying pan until it begins to foam. Remove from the heat and quickly stir in the vinegar. Add the dandelion leaves and seasoning. Return to the heat and turn in the pan for about 20 seconds. Serve immediately.

OMELETTE WITH DANDELION BUDS

SERVES 2
small handful of dandelion buds
1½ oz/40 g/3 tbsp butter
salt and pepper, to taste
4 eggs
2 tbsp/30 ml/3 tbsp water

The dandelion buds should be very tightly closed and should preferably be still bunched together slightly below ground level.

Wash the buds thoroughly and dry. Melt 1 oz/25 g/2 tbsp of the butter in a frying pan and sauté the buds gently for 2–3 minutes. Season with salt and pepper. Put aside and keep warm.

Lightly beat the eggs with the water, and add seasoning. Melt the remainder of the butter in an omelette pan.

Just before the butter changes colour, pour in the eggs. Cook, shaking the pan constantly. Tip the pan towards you and lift the edge of the omelette, then tip the pan away from you to allow the unset egg to run into this space.

When just a little egg remains unset on the surface, add the warm dandelion buds. Fold the omelette in three, and slip it on to a serving dish.

CASSOULETTE DE PIBALLES

Stewed elvers (baby eels)

elvers (baby eels) – allow 7 oz/200 g/ 7 oz per person as a first course
salt
olive oil
garlic cloves, slivered, to taste
dried chillies, crushed, to taste

If the elvers (baby eels) are alive when you buy them, plunge them first into boiling salted water for a few minutes. Rinse and drain. Heat olive oil with slivered pieces of garlic and crushed dried chillies in an earthenware dish. Cook slowly until the garlic is brown and soft. Add the elvers, mix well and serve when hot.

Elvers are traditionally eaten in little earthenware bowls with a wooden fork.

GRATIN DE LÉGUMES

Vegetables in cheese sauce

SERVES 4–6
1 lb mixed vegetables (one-third potatoes, and two-thirds cauliflower, carrots, leeks, fennel, Swiss chard, turnips, celery, and/or celeriac, in any combination)
salt
FOR THE CHEESE SAUCE
1½ oz/40 g/3 tbsp butter
1½ oz/40 g/⅓ cup flour
1¼ pt/750 ml/3 cups milk, warmed
6 oz/175 g/1½ cups Gruyère cheese, grated
2 oz/50 g/½ cup Parmesan cheese, grated
salt and pepper, to taste
freshly grated nutmeg, to taste
handful fresh parsley, chopped
handful fresh chervil, chopped

Boil the vegetables, drain and slice.

While they are cooking, make the cheese sauce. Melt the butter in a heavy-based pan, stir in the flour and cook for a few minutes, stirring constantly. Remove from the heat, and add a little of the warmed milk, stirring constantly. Return to a low heat and continue to add the milk gradually, stirring all the time. Simmer for 5 minutes. Remove from the heat, and beat in most of the cheese, reserving a little. Add salt and pepper, parsley and chervil. Return to the heat and simmer for a further 2–3 minutes, stirring occasionally.

Combine most of the sauce with the vegetables in a gratin dish, and pour the remaining sauce over the top. Sprinkle with the remaining cheese. Bake in the oven at 425°F/ 220°C/mark 7 for 25 minutes, until the gratin is bubbling and golden brown.

NETTLE SOUP

1 lb/450 g/1 lb nettle tops

about 2 oz/50 g/¼ cup butter

3 shallots, skinned and chopped, or spring onions (scallions), trimmed and chopped

1¾ pints/1 litre/1 quart chicken stock

salt and pepper, to taste

1 egg yolk

4 fl oz/120 ml/½ cup cream

Snip off the tops of tender young nettles *only*. (Be sure to wear gloves, for obvious reasons.) Wash thoroughly, using wooden kitchen tongs to turn.

Melt the butter in a saucepan and sauté the shallots. Add the nettle tops, without drying, and sweat for 5–10 minutes until thoroughly wilted. Pour in the chicken stock and simmer for 20 minutes. Cool slightly, then purée in a blender or food processor. Return to the rinsed pan and season.

Mix egg yolk and cream together in a bowl. Ladle in a little hot soup, then stir this back into the pan over a very low heat. Cook for 1–2 minutes, taking care that it does not boil.

LAPIN EN PAPILLOTES

Rabbit baked in parcels

SERVES 4–6

1 young rabbit, prepared

juice of 1 lemon

1–2 tbsp/15–30 ml/1–2 tbsp cold pressed olive oil

salt and pepper

chopped fresh herbs, such as thyme, basil, rosemary, oregano, bay leaf, sage and/or parsley

Cut the rabbit into 6–7 pieces and place in a large bowl. Add the lemon juice, olive oil, seasoning and herbs. Turn the rabbit pieces in this mixture until they are well coated. Wrap in foil or greaseproof (waxed) paper and seal well so no juices can escape. Cook the parcels in the oven at 325°F/170°C/mark 3 for 35 minutes. Alternatively, and much better, cook over hot coals (in which case, wrap in foil).
NOTE: If using herb-seasoned olive oil, this can replace the fresh herbs.

OMELETTE WITH YOUNG GARLIC SHOOTS

SERVES 2–3

1 tbsp/15 ml/1 tbsp duck fat

2 medium potatoes, peeled and diced

4–5 ailettes (young garlic shoots from which the tougher green part has been removed), chopped

6 eggs

2 tbsp/30 ml/3 tbsp milk

salt and pepper, to taste

bunch of parsley, chopped

Heat the duck fat in a frying or omelette pan and sauté the potatoes and ailettes until the potatoes are well browned and thoroughly cooked.

Beat the eggs with the milk and seasoning. Add the parsley, then pour over the potatoes and ailettes. Shake the pan as the omelette cooks.

Tip the pan towards you, lifting the edge of the omelette, then tip the pan away from you to allow the unset egg to run into this space.

When the omelette is cooked but still moist, fold it in three, and slip on to a serving dish.

SPRING SALADS

Chopped garlic and chervil, as well as tender young leaves of dandelions, violets, comfrey, sorrel and borage can be added to salads for a taste of spring. All these plants have tonic and restorative properties.

NINE'S SCONES

12 oz/350 g/3 cups plain (all-purpose) flour

1 tsp/15 ml/1 tsp salt

2 tbsp/30 ml/3 tbsp sugar

1 tbsp/15 ml/1 tbsp baking powder

2 oz/50 g/4 tbsp butter

8 fl oz/250 ml/1 cup milk

Grease a baking sheet. Combine the flour, salt, sugar and baking powder in a bowl. Rub in the butter with your fingertips. Add the milk and work to a firm dough. Place the dough in little mounds of about 1 tbsp/15 ml/1 tbsp each. Bake in the oven at 425°F/220°C/mark 7 for 12–15 minutes or until lightly browned. Serve hot.

MERVEILLES DE MARSAN
Deep-fried pastries

SERVES 6
1 lb/450 g/3½ cups flour
4 eggs
3½ oz/90 g/7 tbsp butter
1 tbsp/15 ml/1 tbsp sugar
pinch of salt
1 tbsp/15 ml/1 tbsp Armagnac or orange blossom water
oil, for deep frying
icing (confectioners') sugar, for dusting

Mix ingredients together in a bowl to form a thick dough. Set aside for 2 hours.

Roll out the dough on a work surface, preferably marble. With a pastry cutter, cut into strips about 1 inch/2.5 cm wide and 3 inches/7.5 cm long. Deep fry in very hot oil. When the pasties puff up, remove and drain. Dust with the icing (confectioners') sugar before eating.

JESSIE'S POUND CAKE

SERVES 6–8
8 oz/225 g/1 cup butter
13 oz/375 g/1⅔ cups brown sugar
5 eggs
8 oz/225 g/2 cups cake flour
2 tsp/10 ml/2 tsp baking powder
½ tsp/2.5ml/½ tsp salt
FOR THE FLAVOURING
½ tsp/2.5 ml/½ tsp almond essence (extract) and 1½ tsp/7.5 ml/1½ tsp lemon juice or 2 tbsp/30 ml/3 tbsp wild cherry flavoured Armagnac or grated rind of 2 lemons or 1 orange
6 tbsp/90 ml/7 tbsp orange or lemon juice, if grated rind used for flavouring

Cream the butter and sugar together in a bowl. Add the eggs, one at a time, beating well between each. Add the chosen flavouring. Mix in the flour, baking powder and salt: if using orange or lemon rind, add the orange or lemon juice to the mixture as the flour is incorporated. Place in a cake tin. Bake in the oven at 325°F/170°C/mark 3 for 1–1¼ hours. Test by piercing with a skewer; if it comes out clean, the cake is ready.
NOTE: Pound cake (*quatre-quarts*, or 'four quarters', in French) originally used one pound of each of the four main ingredients: butter, sugar, eggs and flour.

JEAN'S GINGERBREAD

SERVES 8
2½ oz/65 g/5 tbsp butter
4 fl oz/12 ml/½ cup boiling water
5 oz/150 g/1¼ cup plain (all-purpose) flour
2½ oz/65 g/5 tbsp brown sugar
1½ tsp/7.5 ml/1½ tsp baking powder
¾ tsp/4 ml/¾ tsp bicarbonate of soda (baking soda)
½ tsp/2.5 ml/½ tsp salt
½ tsp/2.5 ml/½ tsp ground allspice
¾ tsp/4 ml/¾ tsp ground ginger
¾ tsp/4 ml/¾ tsp ground cinnamon

Grease and line a cake tin, and grease the paper lining. Place the butter in a bowl and pour in the boiling water to melt it. Add the flour, sugar, baking powder, bicarbonate of soda (baking soda), salt and spices. Beat this mixture very well until creamy. Pour the mixture into the prepared tin. Bake in the oven at 400°F/200°C/mark 6 for 40 minutes. Leave to cool completely before turning out.

· *In the house* ·

Fill the empty hearths with enormous bouquets of tender quince leaves and buds, almond, and shadberry or wild cherry blossoms.

Take some time to draw or paint in watercolour with the children. They especially love doing wild flowers or some other treasure brought back from woodland walks.

HEALTH AND BEAUTY TREATMENTS

Make up various natural health and beauty treatments.

As eggs are plentiful now, make a facial treatment mask with 1 egg yolk, 2 tbsp/30 ml/2 tbsp brewer's yeast and 1 tsp/5 ml/1 tsp olive oil (for dry skin), or 1 egg white whipped with the juice of a lemon (to clear the complexion and firm the skin).

To soften hands mix 1 oz/25 g/½ cup bran or oatmeal with 8 fl oz/250 ml/1 cup boiling water. Leave to macerate for at least 15 minutes, then filter. Soak hands in this mixture as often as possible, especially after washing dishes. Store in the refrigerator.

To improve nails, soak fingertips for 15 minutes in warm olive oil. Keep half a lemon next to the sink and rub on nails each time hands are washed.

Replace morning tea or coffee with an infusion of sage (from the Latin *salvare*, to save or cure) or rosemary for a week or 10 days. Innumerable virtues have been attributed to both plants throughout the ages. A rosemary rinse applied to the hair after shampooing will make it shine; a rinse of sage is said to arrest falling hair and combat dandruff.

To fight against spring lethargy, take daily 2 tsp/10 ml/ 2 tsp honey and 2 tsp/10 ml/ 2 tsp vinegar mixed with a little hot water.

· *In the garden* ·

Start a garden diary of what is sown and planted at this time, noting the temperature and general weather conditions prevailing at the time.

Observe gaps among bulbs and decide where new ones should be put in the following autumn when they will no longer be visible.

Keep a sharp eye out when driving through the countryside or visiting friends' gardens for plants that do especially well or look particularly spectacular, and note them down now with a view to ordering and planting at the end of the year.

Cram silver tumblers full of spring flowers, including wild violets or wood anemones; pale daffodils, such as Mrs. Backhouse or Mount Hood, mixed with trailing leaves of lamium or dead nettle; miniature daffodils with flowering bay laurel or mahonia; tiny bunches of wild red tulips (which at one time covered the fields of Gascony); sloe blossoms and, most delicate of all, tender, pale-green sprays of quince.

Finish pruning roses except for those that flower on the previous year's growth such as true ramblers, many species roses, old roses and some modern shrub roses.

Take advantage of the spring crop of nettles. These are rich in vitamins A and C, protein and trace minerals. Dried and powdered, they are an excellent food supplement for cows, horses, chickens, ducks and turkeys. Newborn chicks and ducklings at Cosmignon are always given a mash of chopped nettles and hardboiled eggs to get them off to a strong start. As nettles also have a high content of nitrogen, they are a valuable addition to the compost pile. After being macerated in a barrel of rain water, they can be used to water and fertilize house plants.

Weather permitting, begin the spring vegetable garden. Plant potatoes, sow carrots, turnips, parsnips, radishes, spinach, beetroot (beets), Swiss chard, parsley and assorted salads. Plant out salad seedlings as well.

All sorts of flowers can now be sown: nasturtiums, morning glory, columbines, cornflowers, sweet William, sunflowers, zinnias, calendulas, larkspur, scabias, love-in-a-mist, California poppies. Most of these are very easy to grow and are great fun for children who want to have their own garden.

APRIL

· *In the kitchen* ·

MOUSSERONS
St George's mushrooms

In a non-stick frying pan, sweat the wild mushrooms known as *mousserons*, or St George's mushrooms, until they give up their juices.

For an omelette, reduce the

juices slightly and pour off the excess into the beaten egg mixture. Pour over the mushrooms and proceed as for omelette with dandelion buds (see page 109). Garnish with a little chervil.

These mushrooms can also be cooked as an accompaniment to roast veal. Or stir cream and an egg yolk into the cooked mushrooms at the last moment and serve on toast.

ROUMILLOUS
Wild asparagus

These tender young wild asparagus can be eaten prepared in the same way as ordinary asparagus – if you have enough. Otherwise they make a wonderful filling for an omelette. Wash them and cut off any tough part of the stalks, but do not peel. Cut into small pieces and sauté gently in butter. Fold into an omelette in same way as for omelette with dandelion buds (see page 109).

POIREAUX DES VIGNES
Wild leeks

Clean and tie the wild leeks in small bunches with kitchen string. Cook in boiling salted water, then drain. Serve warm with vinaigrette dressing.

LOUISIANA SEAFOOD GUMBO WITH CREOLE SAUSAGE

SERVES 10

6 tbsp/90 ml/7 tbsp black roux (see method)

4 oz/100 g/1 cup celery, chopped

4 oz/100 g/1 cup green pepper, seeded and chopped

8 oz/225 g/2 cups onions, skinned and chopped

2 garlic cloves, skinned and chopped

8 oz/225 g/½ lb okra, cut into 1 inch/ 2.5 cm pieces

12 fl oz/350 ml/1½ cups tomato coulis (see page 92)

2 dried red chillies, crumbled

1 bay leaf

fresh thyme, to taste

salt and pepper, to taste

1 lb/450 g/1 lb Creole sausage, in small patties (see page 101)

2 lb/900 g/2 lb shelled uncooked prawns (shrimp), heads and shells reserved

24 oysters

6–8 crab claws or 1 lb/450 g/1 lb crab claw meat

filé powder (ground sassafras leaves), for sprinkling

FOR THE PRAWN (SHRIMP) STOCK

3½ pints/2 litres/2 quarts water

1 onion, skinned

1 garlic clove, skinned

1 celery stalk

salt, to taste

½ lemon

10 peppercorns

5 allspice berries

1 tsp/5 ml/1 tsp coriander seeds

1 tsp/5 ml/1 tsp dill or fennel seeds

3 bay leaves

4 crushed red chillies

1 tsp/5 ml/1 tsp thyme

To make the prawn (shrimp) stock, put the heads and shells of the prawns into a saucepan with the water and the other ingredients for the stock. Cover and simmer for 3–4 hours. Pour through a fine sieve and reserve.

All good Creole recipes begin, 'First make a roux'. A roux is basically a mixture of one part flour and one part fat (vegetable oil, bacon grease, duck fat, etc.) which has been browned to the desired colour – anywhere from pale caramel to black – in a heavy-based pan. The classic method is to heat the fat and slowly incorporate the flour, stirring constantly. Continue stirring on a low heat until the required colour is achieved – for a dark brown or black roux, which seafood gumbo calls for, this takes at least 45 minutes. The last 5 minutes are crucial, as a burned roux must be discarded. Remove the pan from the heat if the roux is cooking too quickly, but continue stirring.

A second method demands a very deft hand but saves time. Heat oil to *smoking* point in a deep, heavy-based pan. Stir in flour gradually, stirring constantly with a long-handled whisk until the roux is dark enough. The roux can be prepared in advance and kept in the refrigerator for several days.

Heat the roux in a saucepan and stir well until thoroughly blended. Stir in the vegetables, except the okra, and cook for 5 minutes. Add the okra, stir well, then stir in the tomato coulis, chillies and herbs. Mix well and stir in hot stock and seasoning. Simmer for 1 hour or longer. This can be prepared in advance as gumbo always tastes better the next day.

To serve, fry the sausages and add with the prawns, oysters and their liquid, and crab to the gumbo. Cook for 5 minutes. Sprinkle with filé powder and serve with steamed rice.

STIR-FRIED TURKEY BREASTS WITH PINE NUTS AND CHILLIES

SERVES 4

3 oz/75 g/¾ cup pine nuts

2 tbsp/30 ml/3 tbsp soy sauce

½ tsp/2.5 ml/½ tsp sugar

1 tbsp/15 ml/1 tbsp Oriental sesame oil

1 tbsp/15 ml/1 tbsp sherry

6 fillets of turkey or chicken breast, minced (ground)

2 tbsp/30 ml/3 tbsp cornflour (cornstarch)

2 egg whites

2 tbsp/30 ml/3 tbsp corn oil

3 small hot chillies, seeded and finely chopped

1 tbsp/15 ml/1 tbsp grated fresh ginger root

coriander leaves, to garnish

1 crisp lettuce, leaves separated

Toast the pine nuts for 10 minutes in the oven at 400°F/ 200°C/mark 6, till golden brown. Combine the soy sauce, sugar, sesame oil and sherry in a bowl and put aside. Coat the turkey in cornflour (cornstarch). Beat the egg whites until frothy, then mix with the turkey.

Heat the corn oil in a wok and stir fry the chilli and ginger for 1 minute. Add the turkey and cook quickly until done. Add the soy sauce mixture and stir quickly. Mix in the toasted pine nuts. Garnish with coriander leaves and place on a bed of lettuce leaves on a large platter. To eat, wrap a few spoonfuls of turkey mixture in a lettuce leaf.

NINA'S CHOCOLATE MOCHA MOUSSE

SERVES 6–8

8 oz/225 g/½ lb bitter cooking chocolate, broken into pieces

1 pint/600 ml/2½ cups double (heavy) cream

4 oz/100 g/½ cup sugar

¼ pint/150 ml/⅝ cup strong black coffee

Melt the chocolate in a double boiler or in a bowl over a pan of hot water. Whip the cream and blend in the sugar. Add the coffee to the melted chocolate, then leave to cool.

Carefully blend the chocolate mixture into the whipped cream. Pour into individual moulds and freeze. Remove from freezer 30 minutes before serving.

MILSTER'S TORTILLA SOUP

SERVES 6

7 corn tortillas

3 tbs/45 ml/4 tbsp corn oil

4 garlic cloves, skinned and chopped

4 oz/100 g/1 cup onion, puréed

¾ pint/450 ml/2 cups tomato coulis (see page 92)

3 pints/1.7 litres/7½ cups home-made chicken stock

1 bay leaf

2–3 tbsp/30–45 ml/3–4 tbsp chilli ancho powder

1 or more hot chillies, to taste

1 tbsp/15 ml/1 tbsp ground cumin

salt, to taste

about ½ lb/225 g/1 cup skinned chicken breast cooked in stock, shredded and cooled

1 avocado, peeled, stoned and diced

4 oz/100 g/1 cup Cheddar or jalapeño cheese, grated

coriander leaves

Cut three tortillas into small pieces, heat the oil in a large saucepan and sauté the tortilla pieces and garlic. Add the onion and cook for 2 minutes. Stir in the tomato coulis, chicken stock, bay leaf, chilli ancho and hot chilli, cumin and salt. Simmer for 30 minutes.

Meanwhile, cut the remaining tortillas into very fine strips. Brush with oil and toast in a hot oven. Add the shredded chicken to the soup. Serve garnished with the avocado, cheese, coriander leaves and toasted tortilla strips.

BRANDADE DE MORUE

Cream of salt cod

SERVES 4–6

12 oz/350 g/¾ lb salt cod, soaked for 24 hours in cold water

1½ lb/700 g/1½ lb potatoes

4 fl oz/120 ml/½ cup olive oil, warmed

4 fl oz/120 ml/½ cup milk, warmed

white pepper, to taste

butter

FOR THE COURT BOUILLON

1 sprig thyme

2–3 bay leaves

1 large onion, skinned

handful parsley sprigs

3–4 garlic cloves, skinned

5¼ pints/3 litres/3 quarts water

While soaking the cod, change the water several times.

For the court bouillon, combine the thyme, bay leaf, onion, parsley, garlic and water. Poach the cod in the court bouillon for 10 minutes. Remove the cod, then cook the potatoes in the same liquid.

Bone the fish, carefully reserving the skin, which makes the *brandade* creamy. Put the fish and skin in the bowl of a food processor and purée. Add the cooked potatoes, one at a time, to the fish alternating with the olive oil and milk until all ingredients have been reduced to a thick creamy purée. (If you don't have a food processor, crush the fish with a wooden spoon, gradually adding the potatoes, milk and oil alternately.) Add more milk and olive oil, if necessary. Season with white pepper. Place the *brandade* in a gratin dish and dot with a little butter. Brown in the oven.

· *In the house* ·

Wait for a sunny day to take the furniture, rugs and cushions outside for a thorough dusting and shaking, while the rooms inside are being cleaned.

Wash windows, mirrors and all glass surfaces. Remove smudges and finger marks by doors, on light switches and elsewhere. Empty fireplaces and wood boxes, and clean them. Replace the split wood in the boxes with summer cushions and picnic rugs. Scrub down kitchen walls. With a feather duster attached to a long pole, remove spider webs.

Air, clean and equip guest-rooms with all necessities in preparation for the spring influx of visitors. Dry clean winter clothes then put away in moth-balls and thyme. Change shelf paper in drawers, and scent with essence of lavender.

Order wine for laying down as well as in anticipation of spring visitors. Fill the house with flowers.

· In the garden ·

Sow sorrel, dill, coriander and parsley for salads, and borage for Pimm's (see page 118). Plant chives, tarragon, summer savoury, oregano, marjolaine, sage, mint, etc. It is impossible to have too many herbs.

Longterm project: design and lay out an old-fashioned knot garden for all sorts of medicinal and culinary herbs.

In the vegetable garden sow green beans, broccoli and cabbages. Plant sets of leeks and lescure and mulhouse onions for winter, and sweet purple onions for summer salads.

In sunny, well-protected seed beds sow tomatoes, melons, cucumbers, all varieties of squash and marrows, aubergines (eggplants), hot and mild peppers, and basil. These will be planted out when the hot weather arrives.

MAY

· In the kitchen ·

SOUPE AUX FÈVES AVEC FARCE

Broad (fava) bean soup with ham-filled omelette

SERVES 6–8
2 tbsp/30 ml/3 tbsp duck fat
3¼ lb/1.5 kg/3¼ lb tender young broad (fava) beans
1 large onion, skinned and chopped
5¼ pints/3 litres/3¼ quarts salted water

5 medium potatoes, peeled and coarsely diced
4 carrots, peeled and coarsely diced
2 turnips, peeled and coarsely diced
bouquet garni, including thyme, 1 fresh garlic shoot, 1 spring (green) onion
FOR THE HAM-FILLED OMELETTE
3 slices Bayonne ham
6 oz/175 g/3 cups fresh breadcrumbs (see method)
handful of parsley
3 garlic cloves, skinned
1 onion, skinned
8 eggs
salt and pepper, to taste
duck fat, for frying

Heat the duck fat in a frying pan and sauté the beans and onion for 5 minutes.

Bring the water to a boil in a large saucepan. Add the beans, onion, potatoes, carrots, turnips and bouquet garni. Cover and simmer while you prepare the omelette filling.

For the omelette filling, chop the ham finely, in a food processor. Scoop out 6 oz/175 g/3 cups of the inside part of a loaf of dry bread and reduce to crumbs in the food processor. Add the parsley, garlic and onion, then chop. Transfer the mixture to a large bowl. Mix in the eggs and seasoning.

Heat duck fat in a large frying pan and gently sauté the omelette. As it cooks, fold over the outside edges to form an omelette shape. Turn this over at least three times to ensure that it will keep its shape when added to the soup.

Slide the omelette gently into the soup, after the soup has cooked for 1 hour. Cook the soup with the omelette in it for a further hour. Serve the soup with the omelette removed. Slice the omelette and eat with pickles and mustard.

CERVELLE D'AGNEAU POCHÉE

Poached lambs' brains

SERVES 4
6 pairs lambs' brains
12 fl oz/350 ml/1½ cups crème fraîche
salt and pepper, to taste
½ tsp/2.5 ml/½ tsp ground coriander
1¼ oz/35 g/1 cup chopped mixed fresh herbs, such as parsley, coriander, chervil, mint, chives
juice of 1 orange
FOR THE COURT BOUILLON
1 onion, stuck with cloves
1 carrot, peeled and sliced
fresh parsley
fresh thyme
1 bay leaf
salt
1 tsp/5 ml/1 tsp coriander seeds
2 tbsp/30 ml/3 tbsp vinegar
FOR THE SPRING VEGETABLES
baby carrots
baby turnips
small, round, white spring onions
peas
new potatoes

Soak the lambs' brains in cold water for 1 hour. Clean, removing the veins and membrane.

For the court bouillon, place the onion, carrot, parsley, thyme, bay leaf, salt, coriander seeds and vinegar in a saucepan. Cook for 20 minutes. Add lambs' brains and poach gently for 12–15 minutes. Drain.

Steam the spring vegetables. Place the brains and vegetables in a serving dish. Warm the crème fraîche in a pan and add seasoning, ground coriander, chopped mixed fresh herbs and orange juice. Remove from the heat immediately, pour over brains and vegetables and serve.

SALADE DE COQUES ET FÈVES

Cockle and broad (fava) bean salad

SERVES 6 AS A FIRST COURSE
2 lb/900 g/2 lb broad (fava) beans
6 ripe tomatoes
2 lb/900 g/2 lb cockles
6 spring (green) onions, trimmed and chopped
hazelnut (filbert) oil
lemon juice
salt and pepper, to taste
oak leaf lettuce, to serve
coriander leaves, to garnish

Plunge the beans in boiling salted water. Remove immediately and slip off the outer skins. Plunge the tomatoes in boiling water. Remove immediately, skin, seed and dice. Steam open the cockles, then remove from their shells.

Mix the cockles, beans, tomatoes and onions together in a bowl. Dress with the oil, lemon juice and seasoning to taste. Serve on a bed of oak leaf lettuce and garnish with coriander leaves. This salad is best eaten slightly warm.

LAPIN AUX COEURS D'ARTICHAUT

Rabbit with artichoke hearts

SERVES 4–6
lemon juice
8 small purple artichoke hearts, pared and cut into quarters
salt and pepper, to taste
1 rabbit, cut in 7–8 pieces, liver reserved
2 tbsp/30 ml/3 tbsp olive oil
1 onion, skinned and chopped
fresh rosemary, to taste
1 bay leaf
1 glass dry white wine
pinch of sugar
1 garlic clove, skinned
6 anchovy fillets, soaked in milk
1 tbsp/15 ml/1 tbsp capers
fresh parsley, to taste

Squeeze a little lemon juice over the artichoke hearts to prevent discoloration.

Season the rabbit well. Heat the oil in a heavy-based casserole and brown the rabbit on both sides. Lower the heat, add the onion, rosemary, bay leaf and artichoke hearts, then cook for 5 minutes. Stir in the wine and sugar. Bring to the boil and cook for 5 minutes. Lower the heat, cover and simmer for about 45 minutes.

Meanwhile, chop the garlic, anchovies, capers, parsley and rabbit liver in a food processor, blender or by hand. When the rabbit is tender, remove from the casserole and keep warm. Add the liver mixture to the casserole and stir well over a very low heat for 5 minutes; do not boil. Pour this over the rabbit.

Serve the dish with freshly cooked tagliatelle.

SORBET AU CHOCOLATE A LA FINE BLANCHE

Chocolate sorbet (sherbet) with Fine Blanche

SERVES 4–6
1 lb/450 g/2 cups sugar
3½ oz/90 g/3½ oz cocoa powder
¼ pint/150 ml/⅝ cup Fine Blanche (an unaged blend of Armagnac)
¾ pint/450 ml/2 cups crème fraîche
3½ oz/90 g/¾ cup icing (confectioners') sugar

Place the sugar and 1 pint/600 ml/2½ cups water in a saucepan and boil for 2 minutes. Add another 16 fl oz/500 ml/2 cups water with the cocoa powder and 1 fl oz/25 ml/⅛ cup of the Fine Blanche. Pour the mixture into freezing trays and freeze. When the mixture begins to freeze and is mushy, mash lightly and return to the freezer. Alternatively, place the mixture in a sorbet (sherbet) maker until it reaches a thick, creamy consistency. Pour into freezing trays and freeze.

Whip the crème fraîche, icing (confectioners') sugar and the remaining Fine Blanche. Serve with the sorbet, which is best when semi-frozen.

WILD CHERRIES IN ARMAGNAC

wild cherries
brown sugar
Armagnac

Wash the cherries, remove the stalks and prick each one wth a needle. Fill a bottle three-quarters full with cherries. Add brown sugar to halfway up the cherries. Fill the bottle with white, unaged Armagnac, and leave for several months. Turn the bottle upside down from time to time. Delicious to drink or use in fruit salads and cakes.

COMPOTE DE CERISES

Cherry compote

SERVES 3–4
1½ lb/700 g/1½ lb cherries, stalks removed
1 lb/450 g/2 cups brown sugar

Choose unblemished cherries and plunge them into boiling water. Remove immediately and place in preserving jars, being careful to fill to the indicated level. Make a thick syrup by boiling 1¾ pints/ 1 litre/1 quart water with the brown sugar. Pour over the cherries to half fill the jars. Close and sterilize at 212°F/ 100°C for 20 minutes. Store the jars in a cool place. Bring out as a winter dessert.

SOUPE DE CERISES

Cherries in syrup

SERVES 6
2 lb/900 g/2 lb cherries
1 stick cinnamon
5 tbsp/75 ml/6 tbsp brown sugar

Wash the cherries and remove the stalks and also the stones (pits).

Place the cherries in a saucepan with half a glass of water, the stick of cinnamon and the brown sugar.

Cover the saucepan and simmer for 20 minutes. Chill before serving.

CHERRY JAM

MAKES ABOUT 3 LB/1.4 KG/3 LB
2¼ lb/1 kg/2¼ lb cherries, prepared weight (see method)
1¼ lb/600 kg/2½ cups sugar

Wash the cherries and remove the stalks and stones (pits). Add the sugar, and leave overnight to macerate.

The next day, cook over a medium heat for 1–1½ hours. Skim off the froth. Pot in jam jars. Sterilize at 212°F/100°C for 20 minutes, if preferred.

CLAFOUTIS DE CERISES

Cherries baked in batter

SERVES 6
1¾ lb/800 g/1¾ lb cherries
butter, for greasing
4 oz/100 g/1 cup plain (all-purpose) flour
pinch of salt
2 tbsp/30 ml/3 tbsp brown sugar, plus extra for sprinkling
3 eggs
8 fl oz/250 ml/1 cup milk

Wash the cherries, remove the stalks but leave the stones, as they add flavour. Place the cherries in a shallow, buttered ovenproof dish.

For the batter, place the flour in a bowl with the salt and sugar, then make a well in the centre. Add the eggs and beat with a whisk, gradually beating in the flour from the sides of the bowl, until the flour has absorbed the eggs. Pour in the milk, stirring continually, until smooth. The batter should be the consistency of a custard sauce. Add more milk if it is too thick. Leave to stand for 2 hours. Pour the batter over the cherries and sprinkle with sugar. Bake in the oven at 400°F/ 200°C/mark 6 for 40–45 minutes. Serve warm.

NOTE: Black cherries are usually used for this classic dish, which comes from the Limousin district of France.

FRED'S MINT JULEP

SERVES 4
handful of mint leaves
1 tbsp/15 ml/1 tbsp icing (confectioners') sugar
bourbon whisky
handful of mint sprigs

Pound together the handful of mint leaves and icing (confectioners') sugar. Add a small amount of water to make a thick syrup. Place a little of this mixture in a silver tumbler and swirl around. Half fill the tumbler with crushed ice. Add bourbon and decorate the mint julep with a sprig of mint.

FINE TONIC

SERVES 1
jigger of Fine Blanche (an unaged blend of Armagnac)
tonic water
juice of ½ lime
twist of lime peel

Pour the jigger of Fine Blanche into a tall glass, add ice cubes and top up with tonic water. Add the lime juice and a twist of lime peel.

ANTHONY PALLISER'S ZEUS COCKTAIL

1 part vodka
1 part Campari
1 part grapefruit juice
twists of orange peel

Stir the vodka, Campari and grapefruit juice together well. Add ice cubes and a twist of orange peel.

VIRGIL THOMPSON'S SAZERAC

small amount absinthe
3 parts bourbon whisky
1 part Cognac
Angostura bitters
Peychaud bitters
lemon peel

Rinse chilled Old-Fashioned glasses with absinthe. Put the bourbon and Cognac in a large glass or jug, with a shake of Angostura and Peychaud bitters. Add lots of ice cubes, and stir well but briefly. Strain into the glasses; they should be about two-thirds or three-quarters full. Rub the edge of each glass with lemon peel.

WHITE EMMANUELLE

4 parts Fine Blanche (an unaged blend of Armagnac)
5 parts Champagne
1 part lime juice
slices of lime, to garnish

Shake well together and serve in champagne glasses, decorated with a thin slice of lime.

PIMM'S

SERVES 1
jigger of Pimm's No. 1
dash of gin
tonic water; fizzy lemonade or champagne-type wine
mint leaves
borage flowers or sweet woodruff
slice of cucumber
slice of orange

Pour the jigger of Pimm's into a large glass. Add a dash of gin and ice cubes and top up with tonic water, lemonade or wine. Decorate with mint leaves, borage flowers or sweet woodruff, and cucumber and orange slices.

· *In the house* ·

After May 11th, day of the three 'Saints de Glace' (Saints of Ice), bring all the delicate pot plants outside for the summer, including the orange, lemon, grapefruit and tangerine trees, stephanotis, jasmine, fuchsia, oleander, plumbago and geraniums.

Try to finish repainting the garden furniture and other chores before the warm weather saps all motivation. Get the pool and tennis courts back in working order; check picnic equipment and refurbish where necessary.

· *In the garden* ·

It is not too late to sow seeds of flowers for cutting in some empty corner of the vegetable garden.

Pick peas and broad beans for freezing and asparagus for bottling.

Towards the end of the month set out heat-loving plants in the vegetable garden: tomatoes, aubergines (eggplants), courgettes (zucchini), melons, cucumbers, mild and hot peppers of all varieties, and basil.

Attack weeds, which are propagating like wildfire. Eliminate them from drives and garden paths with weedkiller or rock salt, and from the vegetable garden and flower beds by hand-weeding or hoeing. Treat vines with Bordeaux mixture and sulphur. Spray fruit trees with a preparation made with macerated tobacco, to eliminate insects. Fertilize roses and spray for mildew and green fly. Garlic planted around the rose bushes should help keep them insect-free.

JUNE

· *In the kitchen* ·

SERGE'S SNAILS WITH WHISKY

SERVES 3
72 snails
rock salt, to prepare
vinegar, to prepare
FOR THE COURT BOUILLON
salt and pepper
thyme
bay leaves
parsley sprigs
cloves
1 onion
1 bottle dry white wine such as Sancerre or Sauvignon Blanc
3½ pints/2 litres/2 quarts pot au feu stock or bouillon
FOR THE STUFFING
10½ oz/290 g/1¼ cups plus 1 tbsp low fat butter
1½ oz/40 g/⅓ cup ground almonds
6 tbsp/90 ml/7 tbsp fresh breadcrumbs, soaked in whisky
7 garlic cloves, skinned and crushed
3 shallots
2 egg yolks
large bunch of parsley, chopped
grated nutmeg
salt and pepper, to taste

Immediately after they have been gathered, the snails must be purged of any bitter or poisonous substance they may have eaten. To do this, place them in a fine mesh wire cage and feed them with thyme, bay leaves and flour for 8 days, watering them regularly. For 3 more days feed the snails only flour, continuing to water from time to time. Place the snails in a large bowl and turn well with a mixture of rock salt and vinegar – this kills them. Leave them in this mixture for 2 hours, stirring from time to time. Wash the snails thoroughly in clean water and put aside.

Cook the snails with the court bouillon ingredients in a bain marie (water bath) over a low heat for 4 hours.

Leave the snails to cool overnight in the court bouillon. In the morning, remove them from their shells, and set aside with 8 fl oz/250 ml/1 cup court bouillon.

Mix all the stuffing ingredients together with the reserved bouillon. In the bottoms of small porcelain cups, place a knob of the stuffing and up to four snails, depending on the size of the cups. (Individual ones are best, but few people have enough of these.) Cover the snails with more of the stuffing. Place the cups in an ovenproof dish.

Bake in the oven at 350°F/180°C/mark 4 for a maximum of 10 minutes. They must not be allowed to bubble for more than 1 minute. Serve immediately, with plenty of bread.

DEVILLED EGGS

SERVES 8–10
15 eggs, hard-boiled
1 tbsp/15 ml/1 tbsp wine vinegar
salt and pepper, to taste
Tabasco sauce, to taste
mayonnaise
paprika
anchovy fillets
crisp bacon or canned red pimiento slices

Halve the eggs lengthwise. Scoop out the yolks and reserve the whites. Mash the yolks with the wine vinegar, seasoning, Tabasco sauce and enough mayonnaise to make a creamy mixture.

Refill the egg whites with this mixture and sprinkle with paprika. Top each egg with a piece of anchovy fillet, some crisp bacon or a small slice of canned red pimiento.

POTATO SALAD

SERVES 8–10
3 lb/1.4 kg/3 lb waxy potatoes
salt
2 tbsp/30 ml/3 tbsp dill vinegar
2 tsp/10 ml/2 tsp mustard
¾ pint/450 ml/2 cups mayonnaise, preferably home-made
1 green pepper, seeded and chopped
1 red pepper, seeded and chopped
1 bunch celery, tender inner stalks only, chopped
3 gherkins (dill pickles)
24 spring (green) onions, trimmed and chopped, or 2 medium red onions, skinned and chopped
12 eggs, hard-boiled and coarsely chopped
1½ oz/40 g/1 cup chopped fresh parsley and dill
nasturtium and borage flowers, to garnish

Cook the potatoes in a saucepan of boiling salted water until just tender. Peel and slice the potatoes into a bowl. Pour over the dill vinegar.

Stir the mustard into the mayonnaise. Gently stir the vegetables, eggs and mayonnaise into the potatoes. Sprinkle with the parsley and dill. Mix well.

Garnish with nasturtium and borage flowers.

119

SOUTHERN FRIED CHICKEN

SERVES 8
2 young chickens (fryers or pullets)
milk, for soaking
flour, for coating
salt and pepper, to taste
oil and fat, for frying (see method)

Cut the chickens into about 12 pieces each. Soak the chicken pieces in milk for 2 hours or more. Drain. In a heavy paper or plastic bag, mix several cups of flour with a generous amount of seasoning.

Heat oil in a deep frying pan (peanut oil mixed with 4 tbsp/60 ml/⅓ cup duck fat for flavour is recommended). The oil should be 1–1½ inches deep and hot enough to turn a 1 inch/2.5 cm square of stale bread golden brown in 1 minute. Shake 5–6 pieces of chicken together in the bag of seasoned flour. Shake off the excess flour. Put into the hot oil, turning after 8–10 minutes. Cook until golden brown and no pink juices flow when pierced with a fork. Drain on absorbent kitchen paper. Add more oil if necessary to maintain the correct level, and heat to proper temperature for each batch of chicken.

PEA SOUP WITH MINT

SERVES 4
3–4 spring (green) onions, trimmed and chopped
4 oz/100 g/½ cup butter
1 lb/450 g/1 lb tender young peas
fresh mint leaves
1 (head) lettuce, shredded
1 tbsp/15 ml/1 tbsp sugar
1 tsp/5 ml/1 tsp salt
white pepper, to taste
1¾ pints/1 litre/1 quart boiling water

Sauté the spring (green) onions in the butter. Add the peas, lettuce and mint leaves, reserving some mint to garnish. Cook gently for about 10 minutes. Stir in the sugar, salt, white pepper and boiling water. Cook until the peas are tender. Cool slightly, then purée in a blender or food processor. Reheat, and garnish with mint leaves.

CHICKEN WITH FORTY CLOVES OF GARLIC

SERVES 4–6
1 chicken, cut into 10–12 pieces
crushed mixed fresh herbs, such as parsley, bay leaves, thyme, rosemary, oregano, sage
salt and pepper, to taste
2 tbsp/30 ml/3 tbsp good olive oil
40 garlic cloves, with skins on
plain (all-purpose) flour, for the dough

Place the chicken pieces in a large ovenproof earthenware casserole. Add the fresh herbs, seasoning and oil. Coat the chicken with this mixture. Place the unskinned garlic cloves among the chicken.

Make a rough dough with flour, water and a little oil. (This will later be discarded.) Roll out and use to seal the casserole (placing an inverted cup in the centre to support the crust if necessary). Cook in the oven at 350°F/180°C/mark 4 for 1½ hours. Break the crust at the table, to release the wonderful aroma of this dish; it can then be discarded. The garlic cloves will be soft and delicious when squeezed out of their skins.

ROAST DUCKLING

SERVES 3–4
1 duckling, about 3 lb/1.4 kg/3 lb
duck fat
salt and pepper, to taste

Place the duckling on a grid in a roasting tin (pan). Smear with duck fat and season with salt and pepper. Roast in the oven at 350°F/180°C/mark 4 for 1–1½ hours, basting every 15 minutes with its juices. Remove the excess fat from the juices and serve.

NOTE: In the Gers, the cavity of the duck is often filled with green olives and slivered garlic before cooking.

JULIE'S TARTE AUX FRAISES
Strawberry tart

SERVES 6–8
FOR THE PASTRY
7 oz/200 g/1¾ cups plain (all-purpose) flour
pinch of salt
2 tbsp/30 ml/3 tbsp milk
2 tbsp/30 ml/3 tbsp sugar
1 egg yolk
5 oz/150 g/½ cup plus 2 tbsp butter, cut into small pieces
FOR THE FILLING
redcurrant jelly
strawberries
crème fraîche, slightly sweetened

For the pastry, place the flour in a large bowl. Make a well in the centre and mix in the salt, milk, sugar and egg yolk. Add the butter and work with fingertips until a smooth dough is obtained. Flatten three times with the palm of the hand. Form into a ball, cover with a cloth and leave for 1 hour in a cool place.

Grease a pie dish that has a removable bottom. Roll out the dough and use to line the pie dish. If it breaks, don't worry; patch with small pieces. Pierce the dough all over with a fork. Bake in the oven at 325°F/170°C/mark 3 for 25 minutes.

While still warm, carefully remove the pastry case (pie crust) from the pie dish. Spread the base with redcurrant jelly. Arrange the strawberries in a circular pattern, starting at the centre. Just before serving, cover with slightly sweetened, lightly whipped crème fraîche.

RASPBERRY ICE

SERVES 4
8 oz/225 g/1 cup sugar
¾ pint/450 ml/2 cups water
lemon juice
10 oz/275 g/2 cups puréed raspberries

Bring sugar and water to the boil, stirring until sugar dissolves. Cook for 5 minutes, then remove from heat. Stir in the lemon juice and fruit. Place in freezing trays and freeze. If you are not using a sorbet (sherbet) maker, stir the mixture vigorously several times during the freezing process. If the sorbet is too hard for serving, soften in the refrigerator for 45 minutes.

SUMMER PUDDING

SERVES 4
1½ lb/700 g/1½ lb mixed red fruits, such as raspberries, strawberries and redcurrants
10 oz/275 g/1¼ cups brown sugar
8 slices white bread, crusts removed

Wash the fruit and place in a saucepan. Add the sugar and cook gently for 5–10 minutes. Line a 1¾ pint/1 litre/4½ cup pudding basin (bowl) with the bread slices, cutting a round to fit the bottom. Pour in the fruit and 6 tbsp/90 ml/7 tbsp of the syrup. Cover with another round of bread. On top of this lay a plate that fits inside the bowl and place a weight on top. Leave overnight in the refrigerator. Unmould the pudding and serve with cream.

STRAWBERRY JAM

MAKES ABOUT 4 LB/1.8 KG/4 LB
3 lb/1.4 kg/3 lb strawberries
2¼ lb/1 kg/4½ cups sugar

Select a warm sunny day for tackling this recipe, which allows the strawberries to conserve their beautiful colour. Choose fresh, unblemished fruit. Wash quickly and carefully to avoid bruising.

Place the fruit and sugar in a saucepan and cook quickly for 25–30 minutes. Take out the strawberries and spread on flat dishes in the sun. Boil the syrup until thick and clear. Put the strawberries into sterilized jars and pour over the hot syrup. Seal. Sterilize at 212°F/100°C for 20 minutes if preferred.

APRICOT JAM

MAKES ABOUT 7 LB/3.2 KG/7 LB
6 lb/2.7 lb/6 lb ripe apricots
3 lb/1.4 kg/6 cups sugar

Wash, halve and remove the stones (pits) from apricots, reserving about 12 stones. Crack and remove the kernels to cook with the apricots. Place the apricots in a deep dish and mix with the sugar. Leave to macerate overnight.

Transfer to a preserving pan and add the kernels. Boil until setting point is reached, stirring regularly to prevent the jam from sticking.

Pot in sterilized jam jars and seal. Sterilize at 212°F/100°C for 20 minutes, if preferred.

PASTIS GASCON
Gascony pastry

The secret of the *pastis gascon* is passed on from generation to generation. It can only be learned through direct experience; even then only a few master the art of making its unbelievably light and flaky pastry dough, which is similar to that of the Moroccan 'bstilla' and undoubtedly a legacy of the Moorish occupation. Between the paper-like layers of pastry

are thinly sliced apples marinated in Armagnac and orange blossom water. Mme Aurensan, the grocer at Lupiac, makes her own brand of this orange essence, which is used to flavour all the *pastis* for miles around. To try this wonderful dessert, one must make the trip to Gascony; to learn to make it, one must stay.

REDCURRANT AND RASPBERRY JELLY

MAKES ABOUT 5 LB/2.3 KG/5 LB
4 lb/1.8 kg/4 lb redcurrants
2 lb/900 g/2 lb raspberries
8 fl oz/250 ml/1 cup water
sugar

Put the redcurrants and raspberries in a preserving pan with the water and heat very gradually to boiling point, stirring occasionally. Simmer for 15 minutes or until soft. Strain through a jelly bag which has been soaked in hot water.

Measure the juice, and to each 1 pint/600 ml/2½ cups, add 1 lb/450 g/1 lb sugar. Return to the rinsed pan and stir frequently until it boils. Boil rapidly for 10 minutes. Test the jelly by dropping a little into a glass of very cold water. When it immediately sinks to the bottom, the jelly is ready. Skim, pour into sterilized jars and seal. Sterilize if preferred.

· In the house ·

Moths, ants, flies and spiders are extremely active at this time of the year. Place crushed mothballs under the edges of all wool carpets vulnerable to moths. Hang mothballs in closets, and replace them in drawers and chests of woollens. Anis and walnut leaves placed in the path of invading ants will repel them. To repel flies, rub wooden surfaces, especially the outside dining table, with essential oil of bay leaves. Burn citronelle candles or incense sticks in the evening to keep mosquitoes away. Oil of pennyroyal will drive away spiders.

· In the garden ·

Sow sweet corn, okra and beans (Tarbais, cocos, flageolets, red and white Spanish beans, and haricots verts). Weed and hoe the vegetable garden thoroughly – very important during this month.

LAVENDER POSIES

Fragrant and attractive lavender posies can be placed among sheets in the linen cupboard and in drawers and closets. Cut the lavender with long stems, just before the flowers open. Tie together in bunches of 15 or so just under the flowers. Bend an uneven number of stems over the flowers and thread a coloured ribbon in and out of the stalks to form a basketweave pattern. Tie up each end with a bow.

LIME (LINDEN) BLOSSOM INFUSIONS

Dried lime (linden) blossoms can be used for infusions all year long. Lime blossom tea is renowned for its calming effect and is usually drunk in the evening before bed. Added to the bath (½ lb/225 g/½ lb of blossoms for 1½ gallons/7 litres/2 gallons of water), it has a sedative effect on nervous or over-excited children.

Pick lime blossoms just as they open and before the pollen begins to fall. Spread them on a clean sheet or on newspapers, and leave in a warm, dry place. Turn them frequently until they are perfectly dry and golden; this takes about 2 weeks. Store in heavy paper bags.

POT-POURRI

Now is a good time to gather herbs and rose petals for pot-pourri. All herbs should be gathered to dry in the early morning before the dew has evaporated and the hot sun has

dissipated their essential oils, which are concentrated during the cool hours of the night.

Gather the roses in the morning, after the dew has dried the petals but before the sun is too hot. Choose flowers that are unblemished and heavily scented. Remove the petals one by one, and place them on a newspaper to dry, in a warm room out of draughts and direct sunlight. Turn them every day. When the petals are competely dry, add a blend of herbs and spices, such as lavender, rose geranium and lemon verbena, lemon and orange peel, and a stick of cinnamon. 1 tsp/5 ml/1 tsp each of *quatre épices* ('four spices' – a mixture of white pepper, cloves, ginger and nutmeg), orris root and Armagnac could also be added for every ¾ pint/500 ml/2 cups rose petals. Store this mixture in airtight jars for 4–6 weeks. The pot-pourri is now ready to be used. Place in bowls with tops around the house. Remove the tops when you want to scent the house. Add a few drops of Armagnac from time to time.

ROSE WATER

Rose water can be used to soothe sunburned or chapped skin or as an eye wash. Choose heavily scented roses (especially of the Gallica family) – preferably red or pink, as these colour the water. Pick 1 lb/450 g/1 lb of petals and put in an earthenware casserole. Cover with cold rainwater or flat mineral water. Place in a hot oven and bring to boiling point. Cool, filter and bottle. This preparation will last for a few days if stored in a cool place.

JULY

· *In the kitchen* ·

ANDREA'S PRAWN (SHRIMP), CHERRY TOMATO AND GOAT'S CHEESE SALAD

SERVES 4 AS A FIRST COURSE

5 tbsp/75 ml/6 tbsp virgin olive oil

2 garlic cloves, skinned and crushed

1 lb/450 g/1 lb raw, shelled prawns (shrimp)

fresh basil, to taste

8 oz/225 g/2 cups cherry tomatoes

1½ tbsp/25 ml/2 tbsp red wine vinegar

8 oz/225 g/½ lb fresh goat's cheese

mesclun salad (see page 93)

salt and pepper, to taste

Heat 2–3 tbsp/30–45 ml/3–4 tbsp of the oil in a pan and sauté the garlic. Add the prawns (shrimp) and cook for about 5 minutes until they become opaque. Add the rest of the olive oil, the basil and the cherry tomatoes. Cook for 1–2 minutes, stirring gently. Add the vinegar and cook for 1 minute.

Crumble the goat's cheese into the salad. Pour the hot prawn (shrimp) mixture over the salad. Season to taste, toss and serve immediately.

HERB-FLAVOURED OLIVE OIL

MAKES 3½ PINTS/2 LITRES/ 2 QUARTS

6 stalks of basil
or
6 stalks of tarragon
or
10 jalapeño or serrano chillies, seeded and crushed

4 garlic cloves, skinned and lightly crushed (omit if using tarragon)

3½ pints/2 litres/2 quarts virgin olive oil

Wash the herbs, if using, and allow to dry. In a 3½ pint/ 2 litre/2 quart bottle that seals hermetically, place the dry herbs or chillies and garlic. Fill with olive oil. Seal and leave to macerate for at least 1 month before using. Use to flavour salads, pastas or ratatouilles or to brush on to meat before grilling (broiling).

COURGETTES A LA CRÈME

Creamed courgettes (zucchini)

SERVES 4

3 medium-sized fresh, firm courgettes (zucchini)

salt and freshly ground pepper, to taste

8 fl oz/250 ml/1 cup crème fraîche

Cut the courgettes (zucchini) into matchsticks by hand or in a food processor. Plunge them into a pan of boiling salted water. When the water comes to a boil again, remove from heat and drain immediately. Leave the courgettes in the colander, covered with absorbent kitchen paper and a weight, for several hours.

Just before serving, place the courgettes in a heavy-based saucepan and mix with the crème fraîche and a little seasoning. Heat gently and stir until the mixture makes a plopping sound; do not boil. Remove from the heat immediately and serve. This recipe brings out the flavour of the courgettes beautifully.

SEVICHE OF TUNA

SERVES 4–6

1 lb/450 g/1 lb fresh tuna

1 onion, skinned and very finely sliced

2–3 chillies, seeded and very finely chopped

6–8 limes

salt

olive oil

fresh coriander leaves

1 avocado, peeled, stoned (pitted) and diced

2 large tomatoes, skinned, seeded and diced

Remove the skin and bones from the tuna. Cut into small pieces and place in an earthenware dish. Add the onion and chillies, and cover with the lime juice. Cover and chill for at least 2 hours.

Before serving, season with salt and add a drop of olive oil. Sprinkle with coriander leaves, diced avocado and tomatoes.

NOTE: Lemon juice may be used instead of lime juice, but it isn't as good.

GAZPACHO

SERVES 4–6

2 lb/900 g/2 lb ripe tomatoes

2 hard-boiled eggs, separated

1 tsp/5 ml/1 tsp dry mustard

3 tbsp/45 ml/4 tbsp olive oil

2 garlic cloves, skinned and crushed

1 onion, skinned and grated

fresh basil, to taste

¾ pint/450 ml/2 cups tomato juice

juice of 1 lemon

1 star anise

salt and pepper, to taste

TO SERVE

freshly made hot croûtons

1 cucumber, peeled, seeded and diced

1 onion, skinned and finely chopped

1 green pepper, seeded and finely chopped

Peel and seed tomatoes. Purée in a food processor or pass through a juice extractor.

Pound the egg yolks, mustard and olive oil together. Reserve the egg white for the garnish. Add the garlic, grated onion and basil, and pound until it becomes a thick purée.

Place in a large soup tureen and stir in the tomato purée and juice. Add the lemon juice and star anise. Season to taste and leave to chill overnight. Add more tomato juice or water if a more liquid gazpacho is preferred.

Serve with hot croûtons, diced cucumber, finely chopped onion and green pepper, and chopped egg white.

SPANISH TORTILLA

SERVES 4–6

12 eggs

salt and pepper, to taste

fresh chopped parsley and basil, to taste

milk

3 medium potatoes

olive oil, for frying

1 purple onion, skinned and sliced

1 green or red pepper, seeded and sliced

1 hot pepper

8 oz/225 g/2 cups cherry tomatoes or 3 medium tomatoes, coarsely chopped

Beat the eggs with seasoning and herbs to taste and a little milk. Cook the potatoes in a saucepan of boiling salted water until tender. Drain, dice and add immediately to the egg mixture. Heat the oil in a round or oval flameproof dish that can be placed in the oven, and sauté the onion, pepper and hot pepper until softened. Add the tomatoes to the egg and potato mixture, then pour over the vegetables in the dish.

Cook in the oven at 325°F/ 170°C/mark 3 for 15 minutes or until the eggs are cooked. The tortilla can be eaten hot or cold, cut in wedges. It makes good picnic fare.

HOT PLUM SAUCE

MAKES ABOUT 9–10 PINTS/ 5–5.7 LITRES/5–6 QUARTS

1 gallon/4.5 litres/5 quarts plums, washed and halved

6 onions

½ oz/15 g/½ oz chillies

1¾ pints/1 litre/1 quart white vinegar

1 lb/450 g/1 lb brown sugar cubes

4 oz/100 g/½ cup salt

2 oz/50 g/½ cup ground mustard seeds

1 oz/25 g/¼ cup ground ginger

1 oz/25 g/¼ cup ground allspice

½ oz/15 g/⅛ cup grated nutmeg

½ oz/15 g/⅛ cup ground turmeric

Place the plums, onions, chillies and vinegar in a large saucepan and simmer for 30 minutes. Rub through a sieve. Return to the cleaned pan and add the sugar, salt, mustard seeds, ginger, allspice, nutmeg and turmeric. Simmer for 1 hour. Bottle and seal. Sterilize at 212°F/100°C for 20 minutes, if preferred.

ALEXANDRA'S PEACH COBBLER

about 1 lb/450 g/4 cups peaches, skinned and sliced

4 oz/100g/½ cup brown sugar

1 tbsp/15 ml/1 tbsp lemon juice

3 oz/75 g/½ cup raspberries

FOR THE DOUGH

4 oz/100 g/1 cup plain (all-purpose) flour

½ tsp/2.5 ml/½ tsp salt

1 tbsp/15 ml/1 tbsp sugar

1 tbsp/15 ml/1 tbsp baking powder

3 tbsp/45 ml/4 tbsp butter or margarine

2 fl oz/50 ml/¼ cup milk

1 egg, lightly beaten

2 tbsp/30 ml/3 tbsp brown sugar, for sprinkling

Place the peaches in a baking dish and sprinkle with the sugar and lemon juice. Cook in the oven at 400°F/200°C/mark 6 for 20 minutes.

For the dough, sift the flour, salt, sugar and baking powder together into a bowl. Rub in the butter or margarine until the mixture resembles fine breadcrumbs. Combine the milk and egg, then add to the flour mixture and mix to a dough.

Remove the peaches from the oven and sprinkle with the raspberries. Drop the dough in large spoonfuls over the fruit. Sprinkle with the brown sugar and bake for 15–20 minutes until the top is golden brown. Serve with whipped cream flavoured with cherry Armagnac or Fine Blanche (an unaged blend of Armagnac).

BLACKCURRANT LIQUEUR

MAKES ABOUT 3½ PINTS/2 LITRES/ 2 QUARTS
2 lb/900 g/2 lb blackcurrants, stalks removed
2½ pints/1.4 litres/6 cups robust red wine
a few young blackcurrant leaves
about 1 lb/450 g/2 cups sugar
½ pint/300 ml/1¼ cups unaged Armagnac

Wash the blackcurrants and place in an earthenware jar. Bruise them with a wooden spoon. Add the wine and a handful of tender, young blackcurrant leaves. Cover and leave to macerate for 2 days in a cool place.

Strain through a jelly bag. Weigh the pulp and add the same weight of sugar. Place this mixture in a preserving pan with the strained juice and wine. Bring to the boil and simmer for 10 minutes. Strain through muslin (cheesecloth). Add the Armagnac and bottle. Use to flavour cocktails such as Kir (dry white wine and blackcurrant liqueur).

REINES-CLAUDES À L'ARMAGNAC

Greengage plums in Armagnac

SERVES 12
50 sugar cubes
1¾ pints/1 litre/1 quart unaged Armagnac
50 good-size, slightly under-ripe greengage plums

Place the sugar and Armagnac in a preserving pan and bring to the boil, stirring well to dissolve the sugar.

When boiling point is reached, add the greengages, which have been washed but are left whole with the stalks attached. Allow to *almost* reach boiling point, then remove from the heat. Cover and leave overnight.

The next day, ladle the greengages into large glass jars and cover with the Armagnac and sugar mixture. Seal and store. Serve with the cream.

SPICED TEA

SERVES 20
6½ pints/3.7 litres/4 quarts boiling water
12 tsp/45 ml/12 tsp Earl Grey tea
sugar, to taste
2 heaped tsp/10–15 ml/2 heaped tsp cloves
1 stick of cinnamon
peeled rind and juice of 3 oranges, unsprayed
peeled rind and juice of 2 lemons, unsprayed
peeled rind and juice of 2 grapefruit, unsprayed
sprigs of mint

Pour 5 pints/2.7 litres/12 cups boiling water over the Earl Grey tea and steep for 3–5 minutes. Strain and sweeten to taste. Pour ¾ pint/500 ml/2 cups boiling water over the whole cloves and stick of cinnamon. Leave to cool. Pour ¾ pint/500 ml/2 cups boiling water over the fruit rinds. Leave to cool. Add the fruit juice to the tea, clove and cinnamon water and the water from the rinds. Serve with ice and sprigs of mint. Bottled and refrigerated, this can be kept for several days.

FRANÇOIS'S LIMONADE A L'ANCIENNE

Old-fashioned lemonade

SERVES 6
4 lemons, unsprayed
4 oz/100 g/½ cup brown sugar
1¾ pints/1 litre/1 quart water

Peel the lemons without the white pith. Squeeze the lemons and reserve the juice. Place the peel in a heatproof bowl or jug (pitcher) with the sugar. Cover and leave to macerate for 30 minutes.

Bring the water to the boil and pour over the sugar and lemon peel. Cool and add the lemon juice. Chill and serve icy cold with sprigs of mint.

CONFITURE DE MÉNAGE

Mixed fruit jam

MAKES ABOUT 6 LB/2.7 KG/6 LB
1 lb/450 g/1 lb greengage plums
1 lb/450 g/1 lb peaches
1 lb/450 g/1 lb apricots
1 lb/450 g/1 lb mirabelles (cherry plums)
4 lb/1.8 kg/4 lb brown sugar

Wash the fruit and remove the stones (pits). Place the fruit in a preserving pan and add the sugar. Stir well and cook over a medium heat for about 45 minutes until setting point is reached. Pot and seal.

SORBET FLAVOURED WITH BLACKCURRANT LEAVES

SERVES 4
8 oz/225 g/1 cup sugar
¾ pint/450 ml/2 cups water
juice of 4 lemons
1 cup tender, young blackcurrant leaves

Place the sugar and water in a saucepan and bring to the boil, stirring until the sugar dissolves. Cook for 5 minutes, then remove from the heat.

Add the lemon juice and blackcurrant leaves. Leave to infuse for 2 hours. Strain. Pour the liquid into freezing trays and freeze.

If you are not using a sorbet (sherbet) maker, you will need to stir the mixture vigorously several times during the freezing process.

If the sorbet is too hard for serving, allow to soften in the refrigerator for 45 minutes.

BLACKCURRANT SYRUP

MAKES ABOUT 3½–5 PINTS/2–3 LITRES/2–3 QUARTS
5 lb/2.3 kg/5 lb blackcurrants, slightly under-ripe
2 lb/900 g/2 lb brown sugar
8 fl oz/250 ml/1 cup water

Wash the blackcurrants and place in an earthenware jar with the sugar. Bruise them with a wooden spoon. Cover and leave overnight.

The next day, stir the fruit and add the water. Place in a bain marie (water bath) and cook gently for 2½ hours. Strain the liquor through muslin (cheesecloth). Boil the syrup for 5–10 minutes. Bottle. To sterilize, place the unsealed bottles in a pan of water up to their necks. Heat gradually until the water is *just below* boiling point. Remove the bottles carefully and seal.

BLACKCURRANT JAM

MAKES ABOUT 15–18 LB/7–8 KG/15–18 LB
8 lb/3.6 kg/8 lb blackcurrants, stalks removed
2½ pints/1.4 litres/6 cups water
12 lbs/5.5 kg/12 lb brown sugar

Wash the blackcurrants. Put into a preserving pan with the water and stir over a low heat until the fruit becomes soft and the liquid has reduced by a third. Stir frequently to avoid sticking.

Warm the sugar and stir in until dissolved. Boil vigorously, stirring frequently, for about 15 minutes or until setting point is reached. Pot in sterilized jars and seal. Sterilize at 212°F/100°C for 20 minutes, if preferred.

· In the house ·

Begin the preparations for August guests. Freeze plenty of fresh country loaves for emergencies. Get in a good supply of pretty paper napkins and candles for hurricane lamps and lanterns. Buy lots of good light wine, and bottle in plain dark green magnums that have been saved for this purpose.

Make sure the guest rooms are well equipped: a bedside tray with iced water, and mint cordial, sugar and a glass; flowers; a choice of reading matter, including something about the region; writing paper, envelopes, stamps, pens and pencils; enough coat hangers (especially the type for trousers and skirts); ash tray, candle and matches, small sewing kit; essence of citronelle or some other insect repellent; a clock. In the bathroom provide sufficient towels including linen face towels and a bathrobe; toothpaste, fresh soap, scented bath essence, cotton, talcum powder, tissues, nail file, eau de cologne, disposable razors.

· In the garden ·

Lift potatoes and leave them for a day or so to dry in the sun, before storing them in a dark, dry place. Gather the ripe stalks of wheat, barley and oats for bouquets. Fertilize the roses. Mulch tomatoes, peppers, courgettes (zucchini), aubergines (eggplants), cucumbers and melons to help keep them moist during the hot dry weather. Cut one barely-open magnolia flower with a few shiny leaves attached, and place in a vase to scent an entire room. Ephemeral – but heavenly.

AUGUST

· In the kitchen ·

SÉBASTIEN'S AUBERGINE (EGGPLANT) PASTA

aubergines (eggplants)
spaghetti
salt
olive oil
pepper, to taste
tomato coulis (see page 92)
cayenne
chopped fresh herbs, such as parsley and basil
grated Parmesan cheese, for sprinkling (optional)

Use equal weights of aubergines (eggplants) and dry spaghetti.

Dice the aubergines into 1 inch/2.5 cm chunks. Salt and leave for 1–2 hours. Rinse, drain and dry the aubergines on absorbent kitchen paper.

Fry the aubergines in batches in olive oil until golden brown. Add pepper to taste. Put the aubergines aside but do not drain off the excess oil. The aubergines can be prepared well in advance and need not be kept hot.

While the spaghetti is cooking, heat sufficient tomato coulis with a pinch of cayenne. Pour over the spaghetti, and top with aubergine and herbs.

Sprinkle with grated Parmesan cheese if liked.

PASTA SALAD WITH TOMATOES, BASIL AND GARLIC

shell pasta (conchiglie)
tomatoes
olive oil
salt and pepper, to taste
garlic cloves, skinned and chopped
chopped fresh herbs, such as parsley and basil

Skin, seed and chop twice the weight of ripe tomatoes as dry pasta. Cook the pasta in boiling salted water until 'al dente', then drain. Add the remaining ingredients and seasoning. Serve immediately, slightly warm or cold.

CROÛTONS GRILLÉS A LA TOMATE
Grilled (broiled) tomato croûtons

French bread
olive oil
tomatoes
chopped fresh basil
garlic cloves, skinned and chopped
salt, to taste

Toast large slices of French bread in the oven at 325°F/ 170°C/mark 3 or under the grill (broiler). Drizzle with olive oil on both sides. Skin, seed and dice tomatoes. Place on the toast and sprinkle with chopped fresh basil, garlic and salt. Place under the grill or heat in the oven for 1–2 minutes.

AUBERGINE (EGGPLANT) PURÉE WITH YOGURT

SERVES 4–6
2 medium aubergines (eggplants)
lemon juice
½ pint/300 ml/1¼ cups natural (plain) yogurt
1 Spanish onion, skinned and finely chopped
chopped fresh mint
salt and pepper, to taste

Bake the aubergines (eggplants) in the oven at 425°F/ 220°C/mark 7 until tender. Cut open and scrape out the flesh into a bowl.

Squeeze a little lemon juice over the aubergine flesh, mash and leave to cool.

Meanwhile, whip the yogurt until creamy. Add to the aubergine mixture with the onion, mint and seasoning to taste.

SQUID, POTATO AND ONION SALAD WITH AÏOLI

SERVES 6–8
2 lb/900 g/2 lb potatoes
2 lb/900 g/2 lb squid, cleaned
spicy court bouillon (see page 119)
12 spring (green) onions, trimmed and sliced
aïoli (see page 128)
salt and pepper, to taste

Cook the potatoes in a saucepan of boiling salted water until just tender. Drain and slice. Poach the squid in the spicy court bouillon. Slice and add to the potatoes with the spring (green) onions. Mix together with *Aïoli*, season and serve warm.

SOUPE DU MOIS D'AOÛT

August soup

SERVES 4
1 cucumber, peeled and thinly sliced
2 onions, skinned and thinly sliced
1 tbsp/15 ml/1 tbsp olive oil
3 tbsp/45 ml/4 tbsp vinegar
¾ pint/450 ml/2 cups natural (plain) yogurt
chopped fresh mixed herbs, such as thyme, chervil and chives
salt and pepper, to taste

Combine the cucumber slices, onions, oil, vinegar, yogurt, herbs, seasoning and 1 tray of ice cubes in a bowl. Chill. Add more yogurt, if needed.

AÏOLI

Garlic mayonnaise

SERVES 6–8
10 garlic cloves, skinned
1 egg yolk
pinch of salt
¾ pint/450 ml/2 cups olive oil
juice of 1 lemon
1 tbsp/15 ml/1 tbsp warm water
pepper, to taste

Pound the garlic with a pestle and mortar. Add the egg yolk and salt. Begin to add the olive oil, drop by drop, stirring constantly as with mayonnaise.

When about 3–4 tbsp/45–60 ml/4–5 tbsp oil have been added, mix in the lemon juice and warm water. Continue beating in the olive oil until absorbed (add a few more drops of water if too thick). Season with freshly ground pepper. Serve with large platters of boiled new potatoes, artichokes and carrots, steamed courgettes (zucchini), hard-boiled eggs, poached cod, squid, winkles (periwinkles) and sea snails.

SOUPE OKROCHKA

Chilled cucumber and yogurt

SERVES 4–6
1 large cucumber, peeled and seeded
1¾ pints/1 litre/1 quart creamy natural (plain) yogurt
salt and pepper, to taste
lemon juice
chopped fresh dill
4 hard-boiled eggs, sliced
8 oz/225 g/1 cup cooked ham, diced – or use canned prawns (shrimps) or crab
¾ pint/450 ml/2 cups sparkling mineral water
dill and slices of cucumber, to garnish

Purée the cucumber and yogurt in a blender. Add seasoning, a little lemon juice, lots of chopped dill, hard-boiled egg, ham and mineral water. Add more yogurt, if needed. Chill. Add ice cubes, garnish with dill and cucumber and serve.

BAGNA CAUDA

SERVES 4–6
4 oz/100 g/¼ lb anchovy fillets
6–8 garlic cloves, skinned
8 fl oz/250 ml/1 cup olive oil
4 fl oz/120 ml/½ cup cream
freshly ground black pepper

Pound the anchovies and garlic together with a pestle and mortar. Heat gently in a pan with the olive oil, cream and pepper.

Serve the bagna cauda in a chafing dish as a dip. Accompany with platters of raw vegetables, such as carrots, fennel, mushrooms, tomatoes, onions, baby artichokes, avocados, broad (fava) beans, celery, asparagus, etc.

VICHYSSOISE

CHILLED LEEK SOUP

SERVES 4
butter, for cooking
3 potatoes, peeled and chopped
1 onion, skinned and chopped
2 lb/900 g/2 lb leeks, white parts only, chopped
salt and pepper, to taste
1¾ pints/1 litre/4 cups water or chicken stock
2 tbsp/30 ml/3 tbsp crème fraîche
chopped chives, to garnish

Melt the butter in a saucepan and sweat the potatoes, onions and leeks with a little water and seasoning to taste for 1½ hours.

Add the water or chicken stock and cook for 5 minutes. Cool slightly, then purée the soup in a blender or food processor. Chill. Add the crème fraîche and garnish with chives, just before serving.

MYRIAM'S AUBERGINE (EGGPLANT) GRATIN

SERVES 4–6

2 lb/900 g/2 lb aubergines (eggplants)

salt

oil, for frying

tomato coulis (see page 92)

grated Parmesan or Gruyère cheese, for sprinkling

Cut the aubergines (eggplants) in ½ inch/1 cm thick lengths. Place in a colander, sprinkle with salt and leave for 30 minutes. Rinse the aubergines and dry them on absorbent kitchen paper.

Heat oil in a frying pan and fry the aubergines. Drain well and place a layer in the base of a gratin dish.

Spoon over a layer of tomato coulis, then a layer of aubergines. Sprinkle with Parmesan or Gruyère. Repeat the layers until the dish is full.

Brown in the oven at 375°F/190°C/mark 5 for 25 minutes. Serve hot or cold.

COLD COMPOTE OF COURGETTES (ZUCCHINI)

SERVES 4–6

olive oil, for frying

3 lb/1.4 kg/3 lb courgettes (zucchini), diced

3 large onions, skinned and chopped

juice of 3 lemons

10 seeds of coriander

salt and pepper, to taste

chopped fresh mint, to garnish

Heat the oil in a pan and sauté the courgettes (zucchini), onions, lemon juice, coriander and

seasoning over a very low heat for 30 minutes. Place in a salad bowl and chill.

Serve the compote very cold, sprinkled with chopped mint.

WATERMELON ICE

SERVES 4–6

1 lb/450 g/4 cups watermelon, diced

4 oz/100 g/½ cup brown sugar

juice of 1 lemon and 1 orange

Purée all ingredients in a food processor or blender. Place in freezing trays and freeze, stirring 2–3 times during freezing.

VIN DE PÊCHE

Peach-leaf cordial

MAKES ABOUT 1¾ PINTS/1 LITRE/ 1 QUART

1¾ pints/1 litre/1 quart good wine

1 glass eau de vie or Fine Blanche (an unaged blend of Armagnac)

40 sugar cubes

peach leaves

1 vanilla pod (bean)

Combine the wine, eau de vie or Fine Blanche, sugar cubes, peach leaves and vanilla. Leave to macerate in a stoneware pot in a dark room for 30 days. Decant and serve or bottle.

PURSLANE AND COD SALAD

salt cod

purslane

oil

lemon juice

pepper, to taste

chopped garlic

Soak a small chunk of salt cod for at least 24 hours in cold water, changing the water at least 3 times. Shred the salt cod and toss with the remaining ingredients.

CHILLED PEACHES IN RASPBERRY SAUCE

peaches

sugar

raspberry jelly

Skin the peaches. Make a syrup with the peach skins, sugar, water and a little raspberry jelly. Poach the peaches in this syrup. Remove the peaches. Reduce the syrup and pour over the peaches. Chill. Serve cold.

PLUM JAM

MAKES ABOUT 10 LB/4.5 KG/10 LB

6 lb/2.7 kg/6 lb plums

¾ pint/450 ml/2 cups water

5 lb/2.3 kg/5 lb brown sugar

Wash, halve and remove the stones (pits) from the plums, reserving about 12 stones. Crack and remove the kernels to cook with the plums. Place the plums, kernels and water in a preserving pan and simmer gently for 45 minutes. Remove from the heat and add the sugar, mixing well. Return to the boil and cook over a high heat until setting point is reached. Pot in sterilized jam jars and seal. Sterilize at 212°F/100°C for 20 minutes, if preferred.

Here are a few cooking tips and general suggestions relating to the kitchen.

★ Always have plenty of tomato coulis (see page 92) and fresh herbs on hand.

★ Whenever possible, skin and seed tomatoes. The difference is comparable to that between caviar and lumpfish roe.

★ Melons are more appealing and easier to eat when peeled, sliced and pre-chilled, and there is nothing to clear away afterwards.

★ Decorate salads with nasturtium and borage flowers, or calendula petals.

★ Always add a little chopped fresh mint to fruit salads.

★ Purée fresh basil leaves with olive oil and freeze. Later this may be used as a base for pesto or to flavour other pasta dishes and salads.

· *In the house* ·

Close windows and shutters during the day to keep out the heat and insects. Keep up the vigil against flying pests. (In Gascony, in case of hornets, one calls the fire department, who will come dressed in space suits to eliminate this menace.)

· *In the garden* ·

The hot dry weather usually lays waste to the more exotic and subtle blossoms but subtlety and exotica are not needed in August flower arrangements. Bright-coloured, simple bouquets look right, such as a large

bowl of nasturtiums, a single passion flower floating in a silver bowl, an assortment of single roses in tiny vases, huge bunches of field flowers and dried grasses, masses of cornflowers, an empty fireplace filled with sunflowers. Zinnias, cosmos, dahlias, calendulas, coreopsis, rudbeckia – all come into their own during the month of August. Just be sure to change the water in vases often in the hot weather.

Now is the time to separate and plant iris, study catalogues and order seeds, plants and bulbs for autumn planting.

Take cuttings from such shrubs and perennials as geraniums, roses, rosemary, santolina, lavender and choisya.

In the vegetable garden, sow spinach, fennel, carrots, turnips and winter radishes (red, black and purple); winter salads such as rocket (arugula), *mesclun*, lamb's lettuce, treviso, endive (chicory); and assorted herbs (dill, coriander, chervil). Plant cabbages, cauliflower, broccoli (especially good are Romanesco and purple-sprouting for spring), Brussels sprouts, leeks, and spring onions. Romaine and sucrine lettuce plants may also be set out. Be sure to have a few cherry tomato plants in the garden; they re-seed themselves happily and produce more than can possibly be consumed.

ACKNOWLEDGMENTS

*The authors wish to thank the following restaurants
for their recipes:*

*Jean-Luc Arnaud of le Bastard in Lectoure (Granité
de Pommes Vertes à la Fine Blanche, page 102 and Sorbet
au Chocolat, page 116)*

*Maurice Coscuella of the Ripa Alta in Plaisance
(Salade de Coques et Fèves, page 116)*

*Marie-Claude Gracia of La Belle Gasconne in Poudenas
(Courgettes à la Crème, page 123)*

---

*I wish to thank my uncle André de Vilmorin and his sister Mapie de
Toulouse-Lautrec, Julie Vietta, Eugène Pineau and Alice Cambus who
taught me the arts of keeping a house, and my friend Pierre Celeyron
who showed me the pleasures of arranging flowers.*
Victoire de Montal

*I would like to thank Georgette Descat who first introduced me to the
cooking of Southwest France, Huguette Lagardère, a wonderful Gascon
cook and great friend, and David Campbell without whose kindness
and enthusiasm this book would not have been written.*
Deborah Roberts

INDEX

Page numbers in italics indicate captions to photographs.